# Biography Today

**Profiles**
**of People**
**of Interest**
**to Young**
**Readers**

Volume 12
Issue 1
January 2003

**Cherie D. Abbey**
*Managing Editor*

D1502588

615 Griswold Street
Detroit, Michigan 48226

Cherie D. Abbey, *Managing Editor*
Kevin Hillstrom and Laurie Hillstrom, *Staff Writers*
Barry Puckett, *Research Associate*
Allison A. Beckett and Linda Strand, *Research Assistants*

Omnigraphics, Inc.

\* \* \*

Matthew P. Barbour, *Senior Vice President*
Kay Gill, *Vice President — Directories*
Kevin Hayes, *Operations Manager*
Leif Gruenberg, *Development Manager*
David P. Bianco, *Marketing Consultant*

\* \* \*

Peter E. Ruffner, *Publisher*
Frederick G. Ruffner, Jr., *Chairman*

This book is printed on acid-free paper meeting the ANSI Z39.48 Standard. The infinity symbol that appears above indicates that the paper in this book meets that standard.

Printed in the United States

INDEXED IN
Children's Magazine Guide

# Contents

3

# Preface

*Biography Today* is a magazine designed and written for the young reader—
ages 9 and above—and covers individuals that librarians and teachers tell
us that young people want to know about most: entertainers, athletes, writers, illustrators, cartoonists, and political leaders.

## The Plan of the Work

The publication was especially created to appeal to young readers in a for-
mat they can enjoy reading and readily understand. Each issue contains ap-
proximately 10 sketches arranged alphabetically. Each entry provides at least
one picture of the individual profiled, and bold-faced rubrics lead the reader
to information on birth, youth, early memories, education, first jobs, mar-
riage and family, career highlights, memorable experiences, hobbies, and
honors and awards. Each of the entries ends with a list of easily accessible
sources designed to lead the student to further reading on the individual and
a current address. Obituary entries are also included, written to provide a
perspective on the individual's entire career. Obituaries are clearly marked
in both the table of contents and at the beginning of the entry.

Biographies are prepared by Omnigraphics editors after extensive research,
utilizing the most current materials available. Those sources that are generally available to students appear in the list of further reading at the end of
the sketch.

## Indexes

A new index now appears in all *Biography Today* publications. In an effort to
make the index easier to use, we have combined the **Name** and **General
Index** into one, called the **Cumulative Index**. This new index contains the
names of all individuals who have appeared in *Biography Today* since the series began. The names appear in bold faced type, followed by the issue in
which they appeared. The General Index also contains the occupations, nationalities, and ethnic and minority origins of individuals profiled. The
General Index is cumulative, including references to all individuals who have
appeared in the *Biography Today* General Series and the *Biography Today*
Special Subject volumes since the series began in 1992.

In a further effort to consolidate and save space, the Birthday and Places of Birth Indexes will be appearing only in the September issue and in the Annual Cumulation.

## Our Advisors

This series was reviewed by an Advisory Board comprised of librarians, children's literature specialists, and reading instructors to ensure that the concept of this publication — to provide a readable and accessible biographical magazine for young readers — was on target. They evaluated the title as it developed, and their suggestions have proved invaluable. Any errors, however, are ours alone. We'd like to list the Advisory Board members, and to thank them for their efforts.

Sandra Arden, *Retired*
Assistant Director
Troy Public Library, Troy, MI

Gail Beaver
University of Michigan School of Information
Ann Arbor, MI

Marilyn Bethel, *Retired*
Broward County Public Library System
Fort Lauderdale, FL

Nancy Bryant
Brookside School Library,
Cranbrook Educational Community
Bloomfield Hills, MI

Cindy Cares
Southfield Public Library
Southfield, MI

Linda Carpino
Detroit Public Library
Detroit, MI

Carol Doll
Wayne State University Library and Information Science Program
Detroit, MI

Helen Gregory
Grosse Pointe Public Library
Grosse Pointe, MI

Jane Klasing, *Retired*
School Board of Broward County
Fort Lauderdale, FL

Marlene Lee
Broward County Public Library System
Fort Lauderdale, FL

Sylvia Mavrogenes
Miami-Dade Public Library System
Miami, FL

Carole J. McCollough
Detroit, MI

Rosemary Orlando
St. Clair Shores Public Library
St. Clair Shores, MI

Renee Schwartz
Broward County Public Library System
Fort Lauderdale, FL

Lee Sprince
Broward West Regional Library
Fort Lauderdale, FL

Susan Stewart, *Retired*
Birney Middle School Reading Laboratory, Southfield, MI

Ethel Stoloff, *Retired*
Birney Middle School Library
Southfield, MI

Our Advisory Board stressed to us that we should not shy away from controversial or unconventional people in our profiles, and we have tried to follow their advice. The Advisory Board also mentioned that the sketches might be useful in reluctant reader and adult literacy programs, and we would value any comments librarians might have about the suitability of our magazine for those purposes.

## Your Comments Are Welcome

Our goal is to be accurate and up-to-date, to give young readers information they can learn from and enjoy. Now we want to know what you think. Take a look at this issue of *Biography Today*, on approval. Write or call me with your comments. We want to provide an excellent source of biographical information for young people. Let us know how you think we're doing.

Cherie Abbey
Managing Editor, *Biography Today*
Omnigraphics, Inc.
615 Griswold Street
Detroit, MI 48226
www.omnigraphics.com

# Congratulations!

Congratulations to the following individuals and libraries, who are receiving a free copy of *Biography Today*, Vol. 12, No. 1 for suggesting people who appear in this issue:

Lauren Darrow, Alpharetta, GA
Susan Hales, Wimberley, TX
Lucille M. Koors, Clarence Farrington Middle School, Indianapolis, IN
Ricza Lopez, Bronx, NY
Rosemary Orlando, St. Clair Shores Public Library, St. Clair Shores, MI
Katey Peck, Vienna, VA
Mimy Poon, San Lorenzo, CA
Tiffany Robertson, Melbourne, FL
Janice P. Saulsby, Dr. Phillips High School, Orlando, FL
Janet A. Speziale, Hilltop Elementary School Library, Lodi, NJ

## Mildred Benson 1905-2002

American Novelist and Journalist
Creator of the "Nancy Drew" Mystery Series

### BIRTH

Mildred Augustine Wirt Benson—known as Millie to her friends—was born on July 10, 1905, in Ladora, Iowa. Her father, J.L. Augustine, was a doctor, and her mother, Lillian (Mattison) Augustine, was a homemaker.

## YOUTH

Throughout her youth, Benson always dreamed of becoming a writer. "I always wanted to be a writer from the time I could walk," she recalled. "'When I grow up I'm going to be a GREAT writer,' I proclaimed to anyone who would listen." Benson published her first story, "The Courtesy," in the *St. Nicholas* children's magazine in 1919. She won a silver badge for her efforts and went on to publish dozens more stories in magazines during her school years.

> "I think that everything I did in my childhood had a terrific impact on what I did [later in life]. I was given quite a bit of freedom. Although my mother tried to make me into a traditional person I resisted that. I was just born wanting to be myself and I couldn't see why girls couldn't do the same thing that boys were allowed to do."

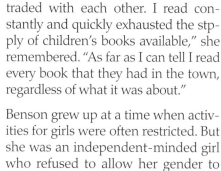

Benson loved to read as a girl. But her book options were limited because her rural Iowa community was too small to support a public library. She had to satisfy her urge to read by borrowing books from friends and neighbors. "Families had their own libraries and traded with each other. I read constantly and quickly exhausted the stpply of children's books available," she remembered. "As far as I can tell I read every book that they had in the town, regardless of what it was about."

Benson grew up at a time when activities for girls were often restricted. But she was an independent-minded girl who refused to allow her gender to determine the types of activities she enjoyed. "I detested dolls, but played with hundreds of tiny wooden spools, moving them as actors on a stage," she noted. Benson also participated in sports — which was somewhat unusual for girls in those days — and became an accomplished swimmer and diver. "I think that everything I did in my childhood had a terrific impact on what I did [later in life]," she stated. "I was given quite a bit of freedom. Although my mother tried to make me into a traditional person I resisted that. I was just born wanting to be myself and I couldn't see why girls couldn't do the same thing that boys were allowed to do."

## EDUCATION

Benson attended the University of Iowa, where she worked on the student newspaper and became a champion diver. She also wrote and sold numer-

*Benson recalled reading constantly when she was young, quickly exhausting the supply of books for children.*

ous short stories during her college years to help pay for her education. After earning her bachelor's degree in English in 1925, Benson spent a year working as a reporter and society editor for the *Clinton Herald,* a newspaper based in Clinton, Iowa. Then she returned to the university to study journalism. "Journalism was just what I was interested in," she explained. "It was opening up for the first time for women back then." In 1927 Benson became first person — male or female — to earn a master's degree from the school of journalism at the University of Iowa.

## CAREER HIGHLIGHTS

Benson wrote more than 130 books between 1927 and 1959. Most of her books were published as part of various popular series aimed at juvenile audiences. She wrote some books under her own name (she was known as Mildred A. Wirt during her career as a novelist), but most of her books were published under pseudonyms (false names used by writers). Benson is best known for creating the enormously popular teenage detective Nancy Drew. Under the pseudonym Carolyn Keene, she wrote 23 of the first 30 books in the "Nancy Drew Mystery" series between 1930 and 1953.

Although several other authors wrote "Nancy Drew" books over the years, Benson is widely acknowledged as the original creator of the character.

In addition to the "Nancy Drew" series, Benson wrote a number of "Dana Girls" mysteries under the pseudonym Carolyn Keene. She also published books in the "Ruth Fielding" series under the pseudonym Alice B. Emerson; the "Kay Tracey" series under the pen name Frances K. Judd; the "Honey Bunch" series as Helen Louise Thorndyke; and the "Dot and Dash" series as Dorothy West. Among the series published under her own name were the "Ruth Darrow Flying Stories" and "Penny Parker Mystery Stories." Benson worked as a journalist throughout the years that she wrote juvenile novels. In 1959 she decided to stop writing novels and concentrate on her career in journalism. She published thousands of newspaper articles and columns during her years as a reporter.

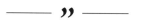

> *"All the books that were handled as series in those days were written under pen names. The reason they did that was so that if an author ceased to write the book, it could be turned over to another author and you do not change the name [on the cover]."*

## Writing for the Stratemeyer Syndicate

After earning her master's degree in journalism, Benson went to work as a reporter for the *Iowa City Press-Citizen*. It was there that she met her first husband, Asa Wirt, who was a correspondent for the Associated Press. In the late 1920s Benson traveled to New York City to look for free-lance writing jobs. She met with Edward Stratemeyer, the head of a publishing company that produced several popular series of juvenile fiction, including the "Bobbsey Twins" and "Hardy Boys" books. Stratemeyer's company, known as the Stratemeyer Syndicate, hired lots of unknown writers to produce the frequent installments in its many series of books. All of these series were published under pseudonyms. "All the books that were handled as series in those days were written under pen names," Benson explained. "The reason they did that was so that if an author ceased to write the book, it could be turned over to another author and you do not change the name [on the cover]."

The people who actually wrote the books for the Stratemeyer Syndicate were bound by the terms of a strict contract. They received a flat fee for their manuscripts, and they gave up all rights to receive royalty payments on future sales of the books. They were not allowed to take credit for the books they wrote for Stratemeyer under pseudonyms. As far as readers knew, "Carolyn Keene" and the other Syndicate pseudonyms were real people. The authors were also forbidden to use the pseudonyms for work published outside of the Syndicate.

## Creating Nancy Drew

Stratemeyer contacted Benson shortly after she returned to Iowa. The publisher asked her to write several books in his established "Ruth Fielding" series under the pseudonym Alice B. Emerson. Pleased with this early work, Stratemeyer invited Benson to write the first few volumes of a new series called "Nancy Drew Mysteries." This series, which would feature a teenage girl detective, was intended as a counterpart to the Syndicate's popular "Hardy Boys" books.

Stratemeyer provided Benson with a one-page outline that included the names of the main characters and the general story line. The writer then expanded upon this information to produce full-length novels featuring a heroine who became one of the most beloved characters in young adult literature. "The plots provided me were brief, yet certain hackneyed [unoriginal] names and situations could not be bypassed," she recalled. "Therefore I concentrated upon Nancy, trying to make her a departure from the stereotyped heroine commonly encountered in series books of the day."

Benson intentionally made Nancy Drew into an idealized character. Nancy was attractive and popular, bold and intelligent, independent and athletic. "I wanted to do something different," Benson explained. "The heroines of girls' books back then were all namby-pamby. I was expressing a sort of tomboy spirit." At first it appeared as if the author had gone too far in creating her heroine. The publisher did not like her version of the character and initially threatened to reject the book. "Mr. Stratemeyer expressed bitter disappointment when he received the first manuscript, *The Secret of the Old Clock,* saying the heroine was much too flip and would never be well received," Benson remembered. But he reluctantly agreed to publish Benson's stories. "When the first three volumes hit the market they were an immediate cash-register success for the syndicate," she recalled triumphantly.

## The "Nancy Drew" Series Becomes a Blockbuster

Benson's character attracted the attention of girls across the country, who scrambled to buy the early volumes in the "Nancy Drew" series. "America's blond-haired, blue-eyed, lock-picking dynamo instantly captured

*A modern cover of* The Secret of the Old Clock, *the first book in the "Nancy Drew" series.*

readers' hearts when the first title in the series, *The Secret of the Old Clock,* was released in 1930," wrote Karen Plunkett-Powell, author of *The Nancy Drew Scrapbook*. "And why not? Unlike the majority of her rather prim, Victorian predecessors, Nancy burst onto the scene early in the Great Depression as a courageous, intelligent, and inspiring heroine."

By 1933 the "Nancy Drew" books were outselling the most popular series of boys' books by a two to one margin. The girl detective became a publishing phenomenon that continues to draw readers 70 years later. The books have sold 100 million volumes and been translated into 17 languages. They have also inspired a television series, several movies, and a variety of products. Benson wrote the first seven volumes of the "Nancy Drew" series, which were published between 1930 and 1932. Then the Stratemeyer Syndicate notified her that, due to financial problems, it wanted to cut her usual payment of $125 in half. Benson refused to accept the lower amount, and another writer (war historian and novelist Walter Karig) produced the next three volumes in the series. But Benson eventually came back to write 16 more "Nancy Drew" books (numbers 11 through 25, and 30). Her last contribution to the series, *The Clue of the Velvet Mask,* was published in 1953.

*Benson intentionally made Nancy Drew into an idealized character who was attractive and popular, bold and intelligent, independent and athletic. "I wanted to do something different. The heroines of girls' books back then were all namby-pamby. I was expressing a sort of tomboy spirit."*

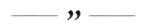

Through the years, the basic facts of the series have remained unchanged. Nancy Drew lives with her doting father, the handsome and wealthy lawyer Carson Drew, in the fictional town of River Heights. Her mother died when she was three, so 16-year-old Nancy is cared for by their German housekeeper, Hannah Gruen. Nancy's best friends are tomboy George (short for Georgina) Fayne and timid Bess Marvin. Her steady boyfriend, Ned Nickerson, is a star athlete at Emerson College. Nancy drives around in her blue roadster, encountering mysteries and solving crimes. She considers herself the equal of any boy and most adults, and insists upon being taken seriously by everyone she meets.

Many fans claim that the key to the series' success is the main character that Benson created in 1930, when Nancy Drew seemed to be ahead of her time. "Before those books came out, literature for girls were entirely a different style," Benson noted. "The most exciting things they put in stories for girls were going to camp or making a trip somewhere. They didn't promote the idea at all that girls could have careers or experiences on an equal level with boys. Girls were ready for that theme. . . . Now that kind of woman is common, but then it was a new concept, though not to me. I just naturally thought that girls could do the things boys did."

*"Before those books came out, literature for girls was entirely a different style. The most exciting things they put in stories for girls were going to camp or making a trip somewhere. They didn't promote the idea at all that girls could have careers or experiences on an equal level with boys. Girls were ready for that theme. . . . Now that kind of woman is common, but then it was a new concept, though not to me. I just naturally thought that girls could do the things boys did."*

## Continuing as a Journalist

During the years when she produced the "Nancy Drew" books, Benson also wrote a number of other books and continued working as a journalist. For the most part, she considered writing novels to be a good way to earn extra money. "It was just a job to do," she admitted. "Some things I liked and some things I did not like. It was a day's work. I did it just like I did my newspaper work. I wrote from early morning to late night for a good many years." In fact, Benson once wrote 13 novels in a single year while also working as a journalist, raising her young daughter, and caring for her husband, who had suffered a stroke. She claimed that she never read any of her books once she had finished them. "Because the minute I do I'm going into the past, and I never dwell on the past," she explained. "I think about what I'm doing today and what I'm going to do tomorrow."

In addition to writing for the "Nancy Drew" series, Benson produced volumes for several other series in the Stratemeyer Syndicate. For example, she wrote 12 books for the "Dana Girls" mystery series under the pseudonym Carolyn Keene. The Dana Girls were younger versions of Nancy Drew who solved mysteries between classes at the Starhurst Boarding School. The popularity of Benson's work for the Syndicate led to opportunities to publish her own stories independently, under her own name. Her favorite was her "Penny Parker" mystery series, which followed the daring adventures of the daughter of a newspaper editor. Benson's novels under her own name were successful enough that in 1936 publisher Cupples and Leon asked her to create her own series. Known as "Mildred A. Wirt Mystery Stories," the series eventually included eight titles.

Benson and her first husband moved from Iowa to Ohio during these years, settling first in Cleveland and then in Toledo. In 1944, during World War II, she began working as a reporter at the *Toledo Times.* She reported on events at city hall and on significant local court cases. She worked hard to prove herself, even though she was certain that she would lose her job at the end of the war, when large numbers of American men started returning from military duty. "I was told after [World War II] ended there would be layoffs and I would be the first one to go," she remembered. "I took the warning seriously and for years I worked with a shadow over my head, never knowing when the last week would come." But the pink slip that she feared never arrived. Instead, she continued working at the paper and its successor, the *Toledo Blade,* for a grand total of 58 years.

Benson's first husband died in 1947. Three years later she married George Benson, who was the editor of the *Toledo Times.* He died in 1959, the same year she published her last novel, *Quarry Ghost.* At this point Benson decided to quit writing novels and concentrate on her career as a journalist. In the late 1960s a publisher approached her about starting a new series of juvenile novels. But Benson realized that she no longer felt connected with the problems of modern teens. "For a moment I was tempted. Plots began to percolate," she remembered. "Then fog settled over my typewriter. The teenagers for whom I wrote lived in a world far removed from drugs, abortion, divorce, and racial clash. Regretfully, I turned down the offer. Any character I might create would never be attuned to today's social problems."

### The Mystery of Nancy Drew's Creator

For 50 years after she wrote the first book in the "Nancy Drew" series, Benson honored the terms of her contract with the Stratemeyer Syndicate and never publicly took credit for her work. As the popularity of the series grew, however, fans began searching for information about Carolyn Keene. As it became clear that Carolyn Keene was a pseudonym, the true identity of the series' author became a big mystery. Some sources claimed that Edward Stratemeyer had written the first three "Nancy Drew" books himself. After Stratemeyer's death in 1930, his daughter Harriet Stratemeyer Adams took charge of the publishing company. Many people assumed

*Benson visited with her alter-ego, Nancy Drew, in the children's department of the Main Library in Toledo, Ohio, 2001.*

that Adams had also taken over writing the Syndicate's most popular series at this time.

In fact, Adams did become more involved with the "Nancy Drew" books over the years. In the late 1940s Benson started noticing differences between her original manuscripts and the published versions of the books. It started out with minor changes of wording, then gradually expanded to include rewriting or deleting whole sections of the text. She suspected that Adams was behind the changes, which were a major factor in Benson's decision to stop writing "Nancy Drew" books in 1953.

**Revealing the Truth**

In 1959 Adams began rewriting the early volumes of the series. The publisher claimed that she was reworking the original stories in order to bring them up to date and eliminate racial stereotypes and other objectionable material. But Benson, along with many "Nancy Drew" fans, felt that Adams also weakened the main character. "She made her into a traditional sort of a heroine," Benson noted. "More of a house type."

During the 1960s Adams became the primary author of new volumes in the "Nancy Drew" series. Around this time, Adams also began claiming in interviews that she had written all of the "Nancy Drew" books from the beginning of the series. Benson, of course, knew that this claim was false. But she continued to honor her contract and did not contradict the publisher's statements. Still, some fans remained curious about the origins of the series. A librarian named Geoffrey S. Lapin conducted research over several years and finally tracked down Benson in 1969. He called her at the *Toledo Blade* offices and asked whether she was the original creator of Nancy Drew. Benson admitted that she had written the early books in the series, but explained that she was sworn to secrecy by the terms of her contract.

The truth behind the mystery of Nancy Drew's creator finally came out in 1980, when the Stratemeyer Syndicate became involved in a highly publicized lawsuit. Adams wanted to change the publisher of the Syndicate's many series of books from Grosset and Dunlap to Simon and Schuster. But Grosset and Dunlap sued to maintain control over the "Nancy Drew" series, arguing that it had contributed to the books' success by providing original illustrations. Benson was called to testify in court to help establish the ownership of the series. She informed the court that she had written many of the early volumes featuring Nancy Drew. Her lawyer produced a number of

*"Years ago, when I tapped out the opening lines of the first Nancy Drew mystery ever written, I never dreamed that I would spend most of my life defending it,"* Benson once wrote. *"Does authorship really matter? Probably not, but loyal Nancy Drew fans, especially the earliest readers, deserve true information, rather than slanted or incorrect publicity statements."*

documents, including letters from Adams, to prove her claim. "Even if I didn't get it across to the court," she stated, "I know who wrote those books, and I set up the form which made Nancy Drew top sellers." Grosset and Dunlap ended up maintaining hardcover print rights to the first 56 titles in the "Nancy Drew" series, while Simon and Schuster received rights to publish all later volumes.

Despite the fact that Benson's authorship had been proven in court, Adams continued to claim that she had written the entire "Nancy Drew" series until her death in 1982. Some periodicals and reference books repeated this false claim through the early 1990s. Adams undoubtedly had an enormous influence on the series. She was an outstanding business-woman whose career was closely linked with the books' success, and she wrote many of the later volumes. But Benson was the person who created the popular main character. "Years ago, when I tapped out the opening lines of the first Nancy Drew mystery ever written, I never dreamed that I would spend most of my life defending it," Benson once wrote. "Does authorship really matter? Probably not, but loyal Nancy Drew fans, especially the earliest readers, deserve true information, rather than slanted or incorrect publicity statements."

——— *"* ———

*"All of [Benson's] tales display a certain crafts-manship, a clear narrative line, and the suspense that Edward Stratemeyer said was essential in books for young readers,"wrote Anita Susan Grossman in the* **San Francisco Chronicle.** *"Many of her stories — long out of print — hold up surprisingly well, with an appeal that is not entirely due to their period charm. Adult collectors of children's books overwhelmingly prefer the old Nancy Drews to the updated, rewritten versions that have come along since 1959."*

——— 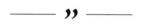 ———

### Celebrating Nancy Drew

Benson finally started receiving public recognition for her role in creating Nancy Drew in the 1990s. In 1993 fans and scholars held an academic conference about the series at the University of Iowa. Benson — now in her late 80s — was invited to take part as a special guest. "All of [Benson's] tales display a certain craftsmanship, a clear narrative line, and the suspense that Edward Stratemeyer said was essential in books for young readers," wrote Anita Susan Grossman in the *San Francisco Chronicle*. "Many of her stories — long out of print — hold up surprisingly well, with an appeal that is not entirely due to their period charm. Adult collectors of children's books overwhelmingly prefer the old Nancy Drews to the updated, rewritten versions that have come along since 1959."

The Iowa conference received a great deal of media attention. Benson was interviewed for a number of sources, including *Good Morning America* and *People* magazine. "I always knew the series would be successful," she said. "I just never expected it to be the blockbuster that it has been. I'm glad that I had that much influence on people." Many experts at the conference

*Nancy Drew has been popular in many different forms for the past 70 years. Here she is shown in a scene from* Nancy Drew, *an original TV movie starring Maggie Lawson as the teenage sleuth. This contemporary version of the mystery series was shown on ABC-TV in December 2002.*

praised the "Nancy Drew" series for providing young women with a role model who gave them the confidence and independence to pursue careers. Others commended the books for helping children learn to enjoy reading.

The conference brought Benson a great deal of public attention. She soon started receiving a huge amount of fan mail at her *Toledo Blade* office. "Most of them identified with [the character of Nancy Drew]. In my fan mail that I receive, they say that they were inspired to go do things for themselves, to go build themselves careers. I think it was incentive to go out in to the world and to become someone as a woman," she noted. "Most of them say, 'Nancy influenced me greatly,' and, you know, 'Today I am a lawyer,' 'I'm a doctor,' 'I'm a judge.' And I get some from boys, too, but mostly from girls." Until her eyesight began to fail, Benson made an effort to write back to all her fans. "I answer each letter, probably because of a throwback to my own kid days when I wrote to movie stars and then hung around the village post office, hoping for a reply," she admitted.

## The Final Chapter

Benson continued working at the *Toledo Blade* during the 1990s, although she gradually scaled back her activities as a reporter. In 1990 she began writing a weekly column called "On the Go with Millie Benson." The column was aimed at active senior citizens, "people who are willing to go out and do things," she explained. "It's slanted toward elderly people, but it covers a wide scope of people, too." In 1997 Benson was diagnosed with lung cancer, but she came back to work the next day. Whenever someone had the nerve to suggest that she retire, she always responded, "Talk to my lawyer."

*"I always knew the series would be successful,"* Benson said. *"I just never expected it to be the blockbuster that it has been. I'm glad that I had that much influence on people."*

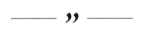

In 2001 Benson became the subject of a 30-minute documentary film, *The Storied Life of Millie Benson,* that aired on Toledo's public television station, WGTE-TV. Health issues forced her reluctantly to enter semi-retirement in January 2002, though she continued to prepare a monthly column for the paper called "Millie Benson's Notebook."

On May 28, 2002, Benson became ill at work and was taken to a Toledo hospital. She died later that evening at the age of 96. She managed to finish her last column, which was about her love of books and libraries, before her death. Her colleagues rushed to honor her contributions to the field of journalism. "Millie Benson was one of the greatest women writers and journalists of the 20th century," said John Robinson Block, editor-in-chief of the *Toledo Blade*. "She was gutsy and daring, a living embodiment of her Nancy Drew heroine. She influenced generations of *Blade* reporters."

The Underwood typewriter Benson used to write the first "Nancy Drew" books now resides in the Smithsonian Institution in Washington, D.C. Her papers, including a personal scrapbook she kept during her youth, form an exhibit at the Iowa Women's Archives in the University of Iowa Library System. "So now it is time for the final chapter, seemingly one destined from the beginning," Benson once wrote. "A fadeout becomes the most difficult of all, for though the story is finished, the reader must be led to believe that the very best lies directly ahead. New worlds to conquer! New horizons to explore!"

*Benson working at her desk at the* Toledo Blade *in the mid-1990s. She continued to work as a journalist until just before her death in 2002.*

## MARRIAGE AND FAMILY

Benson was married twice. In 1928 she married Asa Alvin Wirt, an Associated Press correspondent. They had one daughter, Margaret (known as Peggy), before he died in 1947. Three years later Millie married George A. Benson, a newspaper editor. Her second husband died in 1959. Benson lived in the Old Orchard neighborhood of Toledo until her death in 2002.

## HOBBIES AND OTHER INTERESTS

Benson remained active well into her 90s. She enjoyed swimming and golf for much of her life. She also had a strong interest in archaeology and made several trips to Mexico and Central America to study pre-Columbian cultures. On one trip during the 1960s, she traveled through the remote jungles of Guatemala in a dugout canoe.

Of all her hobbies, flying was Benson's favorite. She first took flying lessons in 1959, following the death of her second husband. "Learning to fly was sort of accidental," she recalled. "I was sent to the airport for a story and they had this $5 promotion going. That $5 promotion cost me hundreds and hundreds of dollars." Benson eventually earned private, commercial, instrument, and seaplane pilot's licenses. She also owned her own plane for many years and logged thousands of hours in the sky.

## SELECTED WRITINGS

*Note:* Mildred Wirt Benson published more than 130 juvenile novels during her career. Many of these works were contributions to series written under various pseudonyms that were also used by other writers. The following list of selected writings focuses on the novels written under her own name and those written under her best-known pseudonym, Carolyn Keene.

### "Nancy Drew Mystery Stories," Under Pseudonym Carolyn Keene

*The Secret of the Old Clock,* 1930
*The Hidden Staircase,* 1930
*The Bungalow Mystery,* 1930
*The Mystery at Lilac Inn,* 1930
*The Secret at Shadow Ranch,* 1930
*The Secret of Red Gate Farm,* 1931
*The Clue in the Diary,* 1932
*The Clue of the Broken Locket,* 1934
*The Message in the Hollow Oak,* 1935
*The Mystery of the Ivory Charm,* 1936
*The Whispering Statue,* 1937
*The Haunted Bridge,* 1937
*The Clue of the Tapping Heels,* 1939
*The Mystery of the Brass Bound Trunk,* 1940
*The Mystery at the Moss-Covered Mansion,* 1941
*The Quest of the Missing Map,* 1942
*The Clue in the Jewel Box,* 1943
*The Secret in the Old Attic,* 1944
*The Clue in the Crumbling Wall,* 1945
*The Mystery of the Tolling Bell,* 1946
*The Clue in the Old Album,* 1947
*The Ghost of Blackwood Hall,* 1948
*The Clue of the Velvet Mask,* 1953

### "Dana Girls Mystery Stories," Under Pseudonym Carolyn Keene

*The Secret at the Hermitage,* 1936
*The Circle of Footprints,* 1937

*The Mystery of the Locked Room,* 1938
*The Clue in the Cobweb,* 1939
*The Secret at the Gatehouse,* 1940
*The Mysterious Fireplace,* 1941
*The Clue of the Rusty Key,* 1942
*The Portrait in the Sand,* 1943
*The Secret in the Old Well,* 1944
*The Clue in the Ivy,* 1952
*The Secret of the Jade Ring,* 1953
*Mystery at the Crossroads,* 1954

## "Penny Parker Mystery Stories," Under Name Mildred A. Wirt

*The Tale of the Witch Doll,* 1939
*The Vanishing Houseboat,* 1939
*Danger at the Drawbridge,* 1940
*Behind the Green Door,* 1940
*The Clue of the Silken Ladder,* 1941
*The Secret Pact,* 1941
*The Clock Strikes Thirteen,* 1942
*The Wishing Well,* 1942
*Ghost Beyond the Gate,* 1943
*Saboteurs on the River,* 1943
*Hoofbeats on the Turnpike,* 1944
*Voice from the Cave,* 1944
*The Guilt of the Brass Thieves,* 1945
*Signal in the Dark,* 1946
*Whispering Walls,* 1946
*Swamp Island,* 1947
*The Cry at Midnight,* 1947

## "Mildred A. Wirt Mystery Stories," Under Name Mildred A. Wirt

*The Clue at Crooked Lane,* 1936
*The Hollow Wall Mystery,* 1936
*The Shadow Stone,* 1937
*The Wooden Shoe Mystery,* 1938
*Through the Moon-Gate Door,* 1938
*Ghost Gables,* 1939
*The Painted Shield,* 1939
*The Mystery of the Laughing Mask,* 1940

## Other Novels, Under Name Mildred A. Wirt

*The Sky Racers,* 1935
*The Twin Ring Mystery,* 1935
*Carolina Castle,* 1936
*Courageous Wings,* 937
*Linda,* 1940
*Pirate Brig,* 1950
*Dangerous Deadline,* 1957 (under name Mildred Wirt Benson)
*Quarry Ghost,* 1959 (under name Mildred Wirt Benson)

## HONORS AND AWARDS

*Boys' Life*-Dodd Mead Prize: 1957, for *Dangerous Deadline*
Ohio Women's Hall of Fame: 1993
Iowa Women's Hall of Fame: 1994
Lifetime Achievement Award (Ohio Newspaper Women's Association):
    1997
Lifetime Achievement Award for Outstanding Journalism (*Toledo Blade*):
    1998
Edgar Allan Poe Special Award (Mystery Writers of America): 2001

## FURTHER READING

### Books

Dyer, Carolyn Stewart, and Nancy Tillman Romalov, eds. *Rediscovering Nancy Drew,* 1995
Kismaric, Carole, and Marvin Heiferman. *The Mysterious Case of Nancy Drew and the Hardy Boys,* 1998
*The 100 Most Popular Young Adult Authors,* 1997
Plunkett-Powell, Karen. *The Nancy Drew Scrapbook,* 1993
*Something about the Author,* Vol. 65, 1991; Vol. 100, 1999
*Writers' Directory,* 1999

### Periodicals

*Detroit News,* Aug. 13, 1971, p.B9
*Editor and Publisher,* June 3, 2002, p.9
*The Lion and the Unicorn,* Vol. 18, No. 1, 1994 (special Nancy Drew edition)
*Los Angeles Times,* May 30, 2002, p.B12; May 31, 2002, p.E1
*Milwaukee Journal Sentinel,* June 9, 2002, p.3

*New York Times*, Apr. 19, 1993, p.A1; May 9, 1993, p.D7; July 11, 1998, p.B7; May 30, 2002, p.A23; June 2, 2002, p.6
*Newsday*, Nov. 18, 1998, p.B6
*People*, Dec. 21, 1998, p.143
*Publishers Weekly*, May 30, 1986, p.30; Sep. 26, 1986, p.12
*USA Today*, Apr. 14, 1993, p.D6
*Washington Post*, May 30, 2002, pp. B7, C1

## Online Articles

http://www.lib.uiowa.edu/spec-coll/Bai/benson.htm
   (*University of Iowa Libraries*, "The Ghost of Ladora," Nov. 1973)
http://www.lib.uiowa.edu/spec-coll/Bai/lapin.htm
   (*University of Iowa Libraries*, "The Ghost of Nancy Drew," Apr. 1989)

## Online Database

*Biography Resource Center Online*, 2002, article from *Contemporary Authors Online*, 2002

## WORLD WIDE WEB SITES

http://www.lib.uiowa.edu/spec-coll/Bai/lapin.htm
http://sdrc.lib.uiowa.edu/iwa/findingaids/html/BensonMildred.htm

## Alexis Bledel 1981-

American Actress
Star of the TV Series "Gilmore Girls" and the Movie
*Tuck Everlasting*

### BIRTH

Alexis Bledel was born in Houston, Texas, on September 16, 1981. Both of her parents are multimedia artists (artists who use audio and video components in their work). Her father, Martin, was born in Argentina, while her mother, Nanette, was born in Mexico. Alexis and her younger brother, Eric, grew up speaking Spanish at home. "It's my first language," she said. "I learned English in school."

## YOUTH

As a young girl, Bledel was terribly shy and never felt as if she fit in. To help her overcome these feelings, her parents encouraged her to become involved in community theater in Houston when she was eight. "My parents felt that theater would help me adjust better," she recalled. Bledel went on to perform in productions of *Our Town, The Wizard of Oz,* and *Aladdin.*

When Bledel was 14, she stopped by a booth at a local mall that was staffed by talent scouts from a modeling agency. The talent scouts liked her look, and she soon began training to work as a model. Part of the training involved reading commercials in front of a video camera. The shy teenager found this part of the process very painful. "It's horrifying to see yourself on video," she explained. "It's unnatural, like having mirrors around you all day."

> "It's horrifying to see yourself on video. It's unnatural, like having mirrors around you all day."

Bledel worked as a catalog model throughout high school, although she admits that she disliked some aspects of modeling. "I hated it because they were constantly telling me to lose weight and to change my appearance," she remembered. "But it was a good way to make money." Her modeling career also gave her the opportunity to travel to some of the world's major cities, like New York, Los Angeles, Tokyo, and Milan. It also brought her closer to her mother, who took time off from her own career to travel with her daughter. "I realized how dedicated she was," Bledel stated. "My mom had put her life on hold to be with me."

## EDUCATION

Bledel graduated from an all-girls Catholic high school in Houston in 1998. "It was my choice to go there because it was a good school," she noted. "And I like being challenged. It was really good for girls to be separated from boys in subjects like math, because statistically they're more apt to raise their hands and speak up." Bledel was an excellent student, except when it came to gym class. She was not athletic and would go to great lengths to avoid participating in gym. "It's not something I'm proud of, but my friend and I would write excuse notes and sign each other's parents' signatures," she admitted.

After graduating from high school, Bledel attended New York University's Tisch School of the Arts for a year. She enjoyed her studies as a film major. "The first year's an overview where you learn about editing, the camera, and writing," she recalled. "I loved it. There are a lot of really creative people, there is a constant exchange of ideas. We talk about what's been done and all the rules for filmmaking and then we talk about how to break them." By the end of her freshman year, Bledel felt certain that her life would revolve around writing or directing films. But a few months later, she left college to pursue an unexpected opportunity as an actress.

> "The whole process of going on auditions and getting cast [for "Gilmore Girls"] took less than a month. It all happened so fast that I didn't really get time to weigh my alternatives. I had really wanted to get a university education. This acting thing had happened accidentally, but still it was one of those opportunities you just can't ignore."

## CAREER HIGHLIGHTS

### Winning a Role in a New TV Series

During her freshman year in college, Bledel had continued modeling and had begun working with a manager. In the fall of 1999, her manager arranged for her to audition for a role in a new television series called "Gilmore Girls." Bledel went to the audition, though she never really expected to land the part. After all, she had very little acting experience. Her career plan at that time was to finish college and then begin working as a director or screenwriter. "I always thought that I would work behind the camera, because it's a more comfortable place for me to be, really," she explained.

To her surprise, Bledel aced her audition and was asked to join the cast of the "Gilmore Girls" in the role of Rory Gilmore, the sweet and intelligent 16-year-old daughter of a single mother. "The whole process of going on auditions and getting cast took less than a month," she recalled. "It all happened so fast that I didn't really get time to weigh my alternatives. I had really wanted to get a university education. This acting thing had happened accidentally, but still it was one of those opportunities you just can't ignore."

*Bledel and Graham from "Gilmore Girls."*

Bledel made the difficult decision to put college on hold and move to Los Angeles, California, to pursue a career as an actress. "I was just worried about leaving school, because I know it's important to have a degree, and I just wanted to make the right decision," she stated. "When you do a pilot for a TV show, you don't know if it's going to work out or not. So I took a little leap of faith that the material was good and that people would like it."

Bledel was initially attracted to "Gilmore Girls" because of the high quality of the script written by series creator Amy Sherman-Palladino. "I thought it was funny. I was laughing out loud when I read it," she remembered. "And there are so many great dramatic elements in the writing, as well as the comedy. You get to see both sides of [Rory's] personality, which is a plus. She's not crying all the time. And it's also not, like, all silly jokes. It's got more of an edge and it's more real, so she seems more realistic."

Sherman-Palladino had auditioned thousands of girls for the part of Rory. She explained that Bledel's lack of acting experience actually helped her land the role. "She's got this angel face. She's just so beautiful," Sherman-Palladino said. "And despite how beautiful she is, Alexis is truly an amaz-

31

ing kid. She's just a good soul. She's got a good heart, and she just doesn't know how good or smart she is. She's just a kid. She's so real. There's nothing false that comes out of her. And she is innocent. I was looking for innocence, and that's something that's really hard to find in kids who work [in show business]. When kids work, they're not so innocent anymore."

*"She's got this angel face. She's just so beautiful," said "Gilmore Girls" creator Amy Sherman-Palladino. "And despite how beautiful she is, Alexis is truly an amazing kid. She's just a good soul. She's got a good heart, and she just doesn't know how good or smart she is. She's just a kid. She's so real. There's nothing false that comes out of her. And she is innocent. I was looking for innocence, and that's something that's really hard to find in kids who work [in show business]. When kids work, they're not so innocent anymore."*

But Bledel's lack of experience — as well as her sudden move across the country from New York to Los Angeles — caused her some problems at first. "It's been really crazy," she acknowledged. "I had to get a car and learn to be a better driver so I can get around LA. Just the basic process of moving has been overwhelming. Then there's all the press and starting shooting and wanting to be good — it's a lot. I'm a mix of emotions — I'm very excited, but at the same time, it's all a lot to take in."

### Starring on "Gilmore Girls"

The first episode of "Gilmore Girls" aired on the WB television network on October 5, 2000. The series centers on the relationship between a single mother, Lorelai Gilmore (played by Lauren Graham), and her daughter, Rory (played by Bledel). They live in the fictional small town of Stars Hollow, Connecticut, where Lorelai works as the manager of an inn. Lorelai became pregnant with Rory when she was 16 years old. She defied her proper, wealthy parents by deciding to have the baby and raise her alone. Mother and daughter have grown up together and share many interests, an addiction to coffee, and even their wardrobes. In fact, the innocent, bookish Rory sometimes seems more mature than her mother.

In the early episodes of the series, Lorelai must go to her parents for money in order to send Rory to an expensive, private high school. Her par-

*The cast of "Gilmore Girls."*

ents agree to pay the tuition, under the condition that Lorelai and Rory come to dinner once a week at their elegant Hartford mansion. The series follows Lorelai's struggle to relate to her parents as well as her own trials as a parent.

During its first season, "Gilmore Girls" aired at 8:00 p.m. on Thursdays, placing it in direct competition with the popular series "Friends" and "Survivor." But the show received rave reviews from critics and soon found a dedicated audience among young women. "'Gilmore Girls' is nothing short of a TV miracle: a family show that's sweet, but not too syrupy, bitingly funny, but not mean-spirited, and fun for viewers of all ages, without appealing to the blandest common denominator," wrote Alan Sepinwall in the *Newark Star-Ledger*. "'Gilmore Girls' seduces viewers with its own fantasy world—well-scrubbed New England town, elegant and happily hip young mom, a general sense of equilibrium—but the cast's chemistry bubbles and the script is exceptional," said John Carman in the *San Francisco Chronicle*.

"Gilmore Girls" went on to be named Outstanding New Series by the TV Critics Association and receive a Viewers for Quality Television Award.

Bledel earned Best Actress honors from the Family Television Awards and the Family Friendly Forum Awards. The show moved to 8:00 p.m. on Tuesday nights during its second season, where its main competition came from "Buffy the Vampire Slayer." It drew an enthusiastic audience of 5.2 million weekly viewers in 2001.

As "Gilmore Girls" began its third season in the fall of 2002, Bledel's character was applying to Harvard University and struggling to decide between her steady boyfriend and the dangerous new boy in town. "It's nice to play a character for so long that I like so much, because it's interesting to see her branch out," she noted. "It's nice to be part of something that you're really proud of. Everyone jokes that I'm too lucky, that the show just kind of caught on, and I haven't had the painful experience of being on something I'm not proud of. But that doesn't mean I appreciate 'Gilmore Girls' any less."

> "[Tuck Everlasting] *is just a great story with a lot of moral dilemmas. It's the kind of great storytelling that's been lost on our generation. It's not showy, in your face, or special effects. It's classic."*

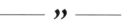

### Appearing in the Film *Tuck Everlasting*

Bledel's strong performance on "Gilmore Girls" led to several offers of roles in movies. "The show has definitely given me opportunities," she noted. "I guess I was sort of surprised but I hadn't had any prior experience with television, so I didn't really know what to expect." Still, the demands of shooting a TV series left Bledel with little time for anything else. She worked on "Gilmore Girls" 14 hours per day, five days per week, for nine months each year. The remaining three months, when the show was on hiatus, was her only chance to pursue film roles.

Bledel's first role on the big screen came in the live-action Walt Disney film *Tuck Everlasting,* which was released in October 2002. The movie was adapted from a best-selling 1975 young adult novel by Natalie Babbitt. (An entry on Babbitt will appear in *Biography Today* in 2003). The book was named one the most important children's books of the 20th century by *School Library Journal,* and it is required reading for many American schoolchildren. "It's just a great story with a lot of moral dilemmas," Bledel explained. "It's the kind of great storytelling that's been lost on our generation. It's not showy, in your face, or special effects. It's classic."

Scenes *from* Tuck Everlasting.
*Above: Bledel and Jesse Tuck, played by Jonathan Jackson.*
*Right: Bledel as Winnie Foster.*
*Below: Bledel with Amy Irving as her controlling mother and Ben Kingsley as The Man in the Yellow Suit.*

In the film version, the story takes place in 1914. Bledel plays Winnie Foster, an independent-minded 15-year-old girl from a wealthy family. "Her parents want her to be a refined young lady," Bledel noted. "And she's not. She's kind of rebellious. She just wants to do her own thing, but she's stifled at every turn by her mother." Bledel was the first person to audition for the role of Winnie. Director Jay Russell claimed that he knew immediately that she was the right person for the part. "When I set out to cast Winnie, I had a feeling that I might never find her. She is in practically every scene. It is her movie," Russell stated. "Alexis Bledel was the very first person I met for the role, and I knew instantly when she walked in the door that she was Winnie. Alexis has a timelessness about her. She doesn't belong to any particular century or any particular year."

In *Tuck Everlasting*, Bledel's character faces a life-changing dilemma. When Winnie learns that her domineering mother is planning to send her away to boarding school, she runs away from home and becomes lost in the woods. She eventually stumbles upon a handsome young man drinking from a beautiful, hidden spring. Jesse Tuck (played by Jonathan Jackson) is the youngest member of a very unusual family, which also includes his father, Angus (played by William Hurt), his mother, Mae (played by Sissy Spacek), and his older brother, Miles (played by Scott Bairstow). The Tucks welcome Winnie into their home and let her in on a secret. By drinking from the magical spring, they have become immortal (they live forever and never die).

Each member of the Tuck family views their immortality differently. The parents see it as a mixed blessing, while the sons' feelings run to opposite extremes. "The different characters react to it differently," Bledel related. "Jesse's character finds so much joy in being able to experience things over and over again, and take trips and see the world, with all the time he has. And then you have Miles' character, who is just tortured by the fact that he's around forever because he's lost his [wife and child]." As Winnie falls in love with Jesse, she must decide whether to drink from the spring and remain with him forever, or return to her normal life. For her part, Bledel claims that she would not choose to drink from the spring. "The film raises a lot of issues regarding the ability to live forever and the darker side of that," she noted. "I just don't think I'd want to see all my friends and family die while I live on."

## Response to the Film

*Tuck Everlasting* received mixed reviews from film critics. Some reviewers praised its sensitive handling of deep issues and claimed that it would appeal to a wide audience. "*Tuck Everlasting*, a sweeping romantic fable about love and mortality, targets an audience of girls in their early teens, but has been made with such skill and sensitivity that its appeal spans generations," said Kevin Thomas in the *Los Angeles Times*. But other reviewers felt that the movie did a poor job of capturing the magic of the novel. "*Tuck Everlasting* is the softest, sorriest excuse for so-called 'inspirational cinema' that Hollywood has produced this year," wrote Craig Outhier in the *Orange County Register*. "It's overnarrated and underwritten, unimaginatively filmed and inflated with gaseous platitudes that rise, helium-like, into a vast and featureless sky of strained morality."

Bledel enjoyed her first film acting experience, although she admitted feeling out of place among big-name actors like Hurt and Spacek. "When I started working on *Tuck* I was this ball of nerves, because here I was with these real actors who had won Academy Awards and everything," she said. "They're all very accomplished and I'm . . . not. But making the movie made me feel like more of an actress, and I can't wait to make another." Bledel also felt a little strange while shooting her early romantic scenes with Jackson. "I had never met Jonathan before the day we filmed our first scene," she noted. "But there I was, dancing around a campfire in a Victorian undergarment in front of a crew I'd just met and kissing an actor I'd just met. That's just one of the absurdities of making movies."

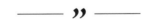

*"I had never met Jonathan Jackson before the day we filmed our first scene. But there I was, dancing around a campfire in a Victorian undergarment in front of a crew I'd just met and kissing an actor I'd just met. That's just one of the absurdities of making movies."*

Despite her success as an actress, Bledel remains uncertain about the future direction of her career. She says that she plans on "making a couple of good movies with good people I can learn from, just to make sure this is what I really want to do for the rest of my life." Starring in a popular TV series and movie has earned Bledel many fans, especially among young women. But she resists the idea of being a role model for teenagers. "There's all this emphasis on actors and entertainers, and there's so much more we could all be paying attention to," she stated. "There are teens volunteering, inventing things, making a difference. Plenty of people do things that are so much more redeeming than what I do, which is pretend to be someone else on a daily basis for entertainment value. Television and movies are a distraction and release for people, which I think is healthy, but there are so many girls out there who are so much more important than entertainers."

## HOME AND FAMILY

Bledel, who is not married, lives in Los Angeles. But she loves her home state and takes every opportunity to visit friends and family in Houston. "It's so refreshing to go home because it puts everything in perspective. When I drive around town, so many buildings I pass are where something happened in my life. Certain neighborhoods are like different phases in my life," she explained. "Texas is like it's own country in a way. Everyone is so friendly. Plus, it has the best barbeque!"

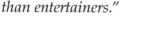

*"There's all this emphasis on actors and entertainers, and there's so much more we could all be paying attention to. There are teens volunteering, inventing things, making a difference. Plenty of people do things that are so much more redeeming than what I do, which is pretend to be someone else on a daily basis for entertainment value. Television and movies are a distraction and release for people, which I think is healthy, but there are so many girls out there who are so much more important than entertainers."*

Bledel remains close to her parents, whom she admires. "My parents are role models because they're strong people," she noted. "They've been very supportive of me my whole life." She claims that her relationship with her mother is different than the relationship between Rory and Lorelai Gilmore, but just as close. "We have much more of a traditional mother-daughter relationship," she stated. "But we can talk about almost anything."

## HOBBIES AND OTHER INTERESTS

Bledel spends her spare time pursuing such relaxing hobbies as reading, writing, hiking, photography, and going to the movies. "Sometimes I feel like I am an old person trapped in a young person's body," she admitted. "I'm boring. I go to movies. I read. That's about it." She also enjoys playing the piano, and she keeps a keyboard in her trailer on the "Gilmore Girls" set. Another of her favorite pastimes is shopping, particularly at Target. "I love Target," she said. "How can anyone not love Target? When I'm bored, I go to Target. When I'm upset, I go to Target. I don't know what it is about Target. If you need something, it turns into 10 things."

## HONORS AND AWARDS

Best Actress (Family Television Awards): 2000, for "Gilmore Girls"
Best Actress in a Drama (Family Friendly Forum): 2002, for "Gilmore Girls"

## FURTHER READING

### Periodicals

*Dayton Daily News,* Oct. 11, 2002, p.C3
*Detroit Free Press,* Oct. 9, 2002, p.F1
*Entertainment Weekly,* Apr. 6, 2001, p.99
*Girls' Life,* Aug./Sep. 2002, p.42
*Houston Chronicle,* Oct. 4, 2000, p.1
*Los Angeles Daily News,* Oct. 9, 2002, p.U4
*Los Angeles Times,* Oct. 11, 2002, p.F12
*Newark (N.J.) Star-Ledger,* Oct. 5, 2000, p.37
*Seventeen,* May 2002, p.144
*Teen People,* June 1, 2002, p.99
*Toronto Sun,* Oct. 9, 2002, p.56
*USA Today,* June 14, 2001, p.D4
*Variety,* Oct. 2, 2000, p.32; Sep. 9, 2002, p.27
*YM,* Mar. 2002, p.94

### Online Articles

http://www.filmmonthly.com/Profiles/Articles/ABledel/ABledel.html
   (*Filmmonthly,* "Life and Love Everlasting for Alexis," Oct. 2, 2002)
http://filmforce.ign.com/articles/373/373676p1.html
   (*Filmforce,* "An Interview with Alexis Bledel," Oct. 8, 2002)

## ADDRESS

Alexis Bledel
"The Gilmore Girls"
4000 Warner Boulevard
Burbank, CA 91522

E-mail: gilmoregirls@talk.thewb.com

## WORLD WIDE WEB SITE

http://www.thewb.com/

## Barry Bonds 1964-

American Professional Baseball Player with the
San Francisco Giants
Holds the Record for Hitting the Most Home Runs
(73) in a Single Season
Five-Time Winner of the National League Most
Valuable Player Award

### BIRTH

Barry Lamar Bonds was born on July 24, 1964, in Riverside,
California. His father, Bobby Bonds, was a professional baseball player. His mother, Patricia (Howard) Bonds, stayed at

home to take care of Barry and his two younger brothers, Bobby Jr. and Ricky.

## YOUTH

A few years after Barry was born, his father signed a contract to play professional baseball for the San Francisco Giants. Bobby Bonds was a very good ballplayer who possessed an unusual combination of speed and power. In fact, he hit 30 home runs and stole 30 bases in five different seasons during his career — more than any other player in baseball history. One of Bobby Bonds's teammates on the Giants was the great Willie Mays, a member of the Hall of Fame who ranks among the all-time leaders in home runs, hits, runs, and runs batted in (RBIs). The elder Bonds and Mays became close friends, and Mays became young Barry's godfather.

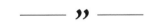

*"He definitely took to baseball at an early age," his mother remembered. "He could hit the ball from the first day he lifted the bat. You'd walk in the door and he'd get a bat and ball and make you pitch to him."*

Barry and his brothers were raised in an upper-class neighborhood in San Carlos, California, a short distance from the Giants' home field, Candlestick Park. Barry's baseball skills became apparent when he was just a boy. "He definitely took to baseball at an early age," his mother remembered. "He could hit the ball from the first day he lifted the bat. You'd walk in the door and he'd get a bat and ball and make you pitch to him." By the time he was two years old, Barry could hit a whiffle ball hard enough to break a window.

When Barry was four, he began accompanying his father to the ballpark. He enjoyed playing in the Giants' clubhouse. Sometimes he would steal sticks of gum from the players' lockers and stuff them into his mouth to make a big wad, like the pros chewed. By the time he was five, Barry was allowed to wear a miniature Giants uniform and shag fly balls in the outfield alongside his father and Mays. He and his brother even signed autographs for their father's young fans. "The cutest thing I remember about Barry in those days was him signing autographs," his mother said. "Barry and Ricky would wait behind the fence outside the clubhouse with all the other youngsters. When kids couldn't get Bobby's autograph, they'd settle for Barry's or Ricky's."

Barry cherished the time he spent with his father at Candlestick Park, because Giants' road games often kept Bobby Bonds away from home. "I really remember more about my mom," Barry noted. "She did everything for me. She always took me to football or baseball practice. She always wrote 'from Dad' on the Christmas presents. My mom was at all the school events. My dad never went. He was playing baseball." Being the son of a professional baseball player created other problems for Barry as well. For example, he had trouble connecting with other kids his age. "You don't know who your friends are at times," he explained. "You don't know if they want to be your friend because you're the son of Bobby Bonds."

——— " ———

*Bonds had trouble connecting with other kids his age. "You don't know who your friends are at times. You don't know if they want to be your friends because you're the son of Bobby Bonds."*

——— " ———

**EDUCATION**

Bonds attended Serra High School, an all-boys Catholic school in San Mateo, California. He was an outstanding athlete who played running back on the football team, guard on the basketball team, and centerfield on the baseball team. But baseball was always his best sport. He led his team to the Central Coast sectional championship three straight years. During his senior year, his batting average was a remarkable .467.

News about Bonds's exploits eventually reached the pros. Before long, professional baseball scouts were coming to see him play. In one game, a scout asked Bonds's coach to let his star player use a wooden bat like the pros used (high school players were allowed to use either wood or aluminum bats, but most chose aluminum because it allowed them to hit the ball farther). Bonds picked out a wooden bat and hit the next pitch over the rightfield wall.

Bonds had a difficult decision to make when he graduated from high school in 1982. He had always planned to go to college, but he was selected by the San Francisco Giants in the major league baseball draft. The team offered him a $70,000 contract to play in their minor league system. Bonds was tempted, but he turned down the money and instead went to Arizona State University on a baseball scholarship.

Bonds was an outstanding player for the Arizona State baseball team. He hit .347 over his three-year career and led the Sun Devils to the College World Series twice, though they were defeated in the championship both

*The Bonds family in the 1970s.*
*From left: Barry, Bobby Jr., Bobby, Patricia, Rick.*

times. During his sophomore year, he tied a National Collegiate Athletic Association (NCAA) record by getting seven straight hits in the College World Series. In his junior year, he hit 23 home runs and was named to the *Sporting News* All-America team.

Although Bonds was one of the best players on the Sun Devils baseball squad, he had trouble getting along with his teammates. He tried kidding around with the guys, but the other players generally viewed him as arrogant and boastful. "I liked the hell out of Barry Bonds," said Arizona State Coach Jim Brock. "Unfortunately, I never saw a teammate care about him. Part of it would be his being rude, inconsiderate, and self-centered. He bragged about the money he turned down, and he popped off about his dad. I don't think he ever figured out what to do to get people to like him." After completing his junior season at Arizona State, Bonds declared himself eligible for the pro baseball draft. He left college in 1985 without completing his bachelor's degree.

## CAREER HIGHLIGHTS

### Major League Baseball — The Pittsburgh Pirates

Bonds was selected sixth overall in the 1985 Major League Baseball draft by the Pittsburgh Pirates. He started out playing for the Pirates' Class A minor league team in Virginia. In professional baseball, most players start in the minor leagues, where they get the training they need to become good enough for a major league team. The Rookie League is the lowest, then Class A, Class AA, up to Class AAA. Bonds started out in Class A, where he hit .299 with 13 home runs. One of his teammates was Bobby Bonilla, who would become one of Bonds's best friends. In 1986 Bonds moved up to the Pirates' Class AAA farm team in Hawaii, where his batting average was .311. But the talented young player did not remain in the minor leagues for long.

One day, Pirates general manager Syd Thrift came to see the Class AAA club take batting practice before a game in Phoenix. Thrift watched as the lefthanded Bonds hit six balls in a row over the rightfield fence. "Any good hitter can do that," the general manager told him. "I'd like to see you hit a few over the leftfield fence." (It is generally considered easier for a left-handed hitter to pull the ball to rightfield. Hitting for power to the opposite field demonstrates true strength.) Bonds proceeded to hit five balls in a row over the leftfield fence. He then turned to Thrift and said, "Is that good enough for you?" Thrift took Bonds back to Pittsburgh with him that night, and the young player remained in the big leagues from that time on.

Bonds made an immediate impact as a rookie with the Pirates. Wearing number 24 like his godfather, Willie Mays, he got a base hit in his first game with the team and logged his first home run within a week. Even though he joined the team two months into the 1986 season, he still managed to lead all rookies in the league with 16 home runs, 36 stolen bases, and 48 RBIs. Unfortunately, the Pirates finished in last place in their division with a 64-98 record. "We may have lost, but we're not losers," Bonds stated. "We're young. We're getting better. In a year, two years, somewhere down the line, we are going to tip the city of Pittsburgh right on its ear."

During the 1987 season, Bonds batted leadoff and switched from centerfield to leftfield. He had another solid season, batting .261 with 25 home runs and 32 stolen bases. The Pirates missed the playoffs again, but the team improved to post a .500 record. In 1988 Bonds raised his batting average to .283 while hitting 24 home runs and stealing 17 bases. Although his numbers were respectable, some people compared him unfavorably to his father and claimed that he was not playing to his full potential. In 1989

*Bonds in 1991, while playing for the Pittsburgh Pirates.*

Bonds hit 19 home runs, one of which broke the major league record of 407 career homers by a father-son combination. His stolen base total remained constant at 32, while his batting average dropped to .248. Once again, the Pirates failed to make the playoffs.

Bonds's contract expired between the 1989 and the 1990 seasons. The Pirates offered him a new contract worth $850,000 per year, while Bonds asked for a salary of $1.6 million per year. When the two sides could not reach an agreement, they took the matter to an arbitrator (an objective third party who listens to arguments on both sides and then makes a binding decision). After the arbitrator sided with the Pirates, Bonds grew determined to prove his worth. "I think Barry is one of those people who has to be challenged—whether it's by his dad, the media, fans, or whoever," said Pirates Manager Jim Leyland. "He's zeroed in and focused more now than any time since he's been here. He's a talented guy. Now he's coming of age."

## National League MVP

Bonds was a solid, dependable player during his first four years with the Pirates, but he was not exceptional. Beginning in 1990, however, he transformed himself into the most productive player in the major leagues and led the Pirates to three straight National League East titles. Bonds's career turnaround came about in an unusual way. "I went to get a haircut," he recalled, "at Fred Tate's barbershop in Pittsburgh. I'm getting my hair cut, and they have the radio on. A guy on the radio says what a great *athlete* Randall Cunningham is, but what a great *quarterback* Joe Montana is. I weighed the two and thought, I'm so bored with having great ability. I want to be a great *player* like Joe Montana. So that haircut was my inspiration. I realized that what I'd been doing— cutting myself short—was wrong. Wrong to me, my team, and even the game. That's when I thought, I'm going to work my tail end off before it becomes too late."

——— " ———

*"I'm getting my hair cut, and they have the radio on. A guy on the radio says what a great* **athlete** *Randall Cunningham is, but what a great* **quarterback** *Joe Montana is. I weighed the two and thought, I'm so bored with having great ability. I want to be a great player like Joe Montana. So that haircut was my inspiration. I realized that what I'd been doing—cutting myself short—was wrong. Wrong to me, my team, and even the game. That's when I thought, I'm going to work my tail end off before it becomes too late."*

——— " ———

Before the 1990 season, Bonds started a weight training program and spent hours running sprints and practicing in the batting cage. He showed up at spring training in the best shape of his life. Recognizing his new strength and power, his coach moved him from leadoff hitter to the fifth spot in the batting order. Bonds felt more comfortable in this key power position in the lineup. He responded by hitting a career-best .301 with 33 home runs and 52 stolen bases. In addition, he improved his slugging average—a measure of a hitter's effectiveness calculated by dividing the total number of bases reached on all hits by the total number of at bats. His slugging average of .565 was the best in the league. He also won a Gold Glove Award for his fielding. At the end of the 1990 season, Bonds was selected as the National League Most Valuable Player and the *Sporting News* Major League Player of the Year. The Pirates finally made the playoffs, but they lost to the Cincinnati Reds in the National League Championship Series (NLCS). The only disappointing aspect of Bonds's phenomenal season was that he hit only .190 in the playoffs.

The 1991 season started off on a bad note for Bonds. Frustrated by losing another contract arbitration hearing during the offseason, he had a highly publicized shouting match with Manager Jim Leyland in spring training. But Bonds overcame the controversy to hit .292 with 25 homers and 43 steals, narrowly missing a second consecutive MVP award. The Pirates made the playoffs again with a 98-64 record, but they lost to the Atlanta Braves in the NLCS. The media began criticizing Bonds for his poor playoff performance, as he hit just .148 over the seven-game series against the Braves.

Bonds was disappointed when his best friend on the Pirates, Bobby Bonilla, was traded before the 1992 season. Bonds signed a one-year contract worth $4.6 million, but he made it clear that he intended to become a free agent at the end of the season. Although Bonds had turned into the biggest star on the Pirates, few people expressed regret that he intended to leave the team. He was not close to any of his teammates besides Bonilla, and many of the players found him to be a negative presence in the clubhouse. In fact, one of his Pirates teammates said that "I'd rather lose without Barry Bonds than win with him."

Over the course of his career with the Pirates, Bonds also developed a terrible relationship with the Pittsburgh media. Reporters criticized him as rude and arrogant. Bonds admitted that he disliked dealing with the press, but claimed that it was only because he was a private person. He expressed anger that reporters characterized him as a bad person, and asked that they judge him instead by his performance on the field. "I'm not a media person. I don't like to answer the same questions. I just like to play baseball. I'm not into the other stuff. I turn down a lot of interviews. It's the United States of America. I have freedom of choice," he stated. "I feel the press puts a stamp on certain players and once they stamp you as a 'bad person' then that's what they feed on and there's nothing you can do about it. I know in my heart the type of ballplayer I am and the type of person I am."

Bonds had another outstanding year in 1992, hitting .311 with 34 home runs and 39 stolen bases and winning another Gold Glove Award. He claimed his second National League MVP honor and was named Associated Press Player of the Year. But disappointment awaited him once again in the playoffs. The Pirates led the Braves in the last inning of the deciding game of the NLCS. Bonds fielded a single to left and threw the ball to home plate. But the throw was too late and the Braves scored the winning run.

*Bonds catches a ball during this World Series game, October 19, 2002.*

### The San Francisco Giants

Following his impressive 1992 season, Bonds attracted a lot of attention in the free agent market. To the star player's delight, the best offer came from his father's old team, the San Francisco Giants. The owner of the Giants, Peter Magowan, offered Bonds a six-year contract worth $44 million, making him the highest-paid player in baseball at that time. In fact, his average salary of $7.3 million per year was more than his father and godfather had earned in their entire careers. "My head blew up like a balloon," he recalled. "I wanted to go to the Empire State building and jump, since I could fly at that point."

Bonds was thrilled to have an opportunity to play for his hometown team. "I have never been more excited to play in a city in my entire life than I am now," he stated. He hoped that joining the Giants would give him a chance to make a fresh start. He even changed his uniform number to 25, his father's old number, since the club had retired Mays's 24. "My [new] teammates really took to me differently," he noted. "It wasn't about how you dressed or what you said—it was about how you play the game. They saw this guy play hard and work out every day. They said, 'This kid doesn't play for the money. He plays to be better than everybody.'" To make the deal even sweeter for Bonds, the Giants also hired his father as the team's batting coach.

Although the Giants had finished 26 games out of first place the previous year, they entered the 1993 season with a crop of good young players and a new manager, Dusty Baker. Bonds showed his determination to contribute by smacking a home run in his first at-bat in a Giants uniform. He went on to post the best season of his career. He became one of the most feared hitters in baseball, posting a .336 average with a league-leading 46 home runs, 123 RBIs, and .677 slugging percentage. At the end of the season, he received his third MVP award. Bonds thus became only the tenth player to win back-to-back MVPs, and the first player to do so with two different teams. Although the Giants improved significantly and won 103 games, they missed the playoffs by one game.

*"I'm not a media person. I don't like to answer the same questions. I just like to play baseball. I'm not into the other stuff. I turn down a lot of interviews. It's the United States of America. I have freedom of choice. I feel the press puts a stamp on certain players and once they stamp you as a 'bad person' then that's what they feed on and there's nothing you can do about it. I know in my heart the type of ballplayer I am and the type of person I am."*

## The Giants Continue to Struggle

The 1994 season ended two months early when a labor dispute between team owners and players led to a strike. Bonds was hitting .312 with 37 home runs and 29 steals when the season concluded. In 1995, some opposing teams decided that the best way to deal with Bonds's impressive skills at the plate was to avoid giving him any good pitches to hit. He ended up leading the league in walks with 120 that year, though he still managed to hit .294. His 33 home runs and 31 stolen bases gave him his third career 30-30 season in those categories. Despite his personal accomplishments, however, the Giants finished in last place in their division.

The Giants remained in the NL West cellar during the 1996 season, but Bonds posted another impressive year. In addition to setting a new league record with 151 walks, he batted .308 with 42 home runs and 40 stolen bases. He thus became only the second player in major league history to post a 40-40 season, and he joined his father, Willie Mays, and Andre

Dawson as the only players to achieve 300 home runs and 300 stolen bases in a career. "It doesn't seem real right now," he said of joining the 300-300 club. "I've still got a lot of years left and it doesn't seem like it should be here that fast."

Prior to the 1997 season, the Giants gave Bonds a two-year contract extension worth $11.5 million per year. The team also made a few roster changes that helped the Giants cruise to a division title and a spot in the playoffs. Unfortunately, they lost to the Florida Marlins in the NLCS. "We're all down, and all losses are tough," Bonds said afterward. "It was very frustrating. We went out there and played hard. They went out there and played hard. They won." Bonds had another good year in 1997, hitting .291 with 40 home runs and 37 stolen bases. This was the fifth 30-30 season of his career, tying the record held by his father. Once again, however, the star player disappeared during the postseason, knocking out only three hits.

*"Everything is perfect in that one particular second,"* Bonds said of his home-run swing. *"It's in slow motion. You don't hear anything, you don't even feel it hit your bat. That's the zone."*

In 1998 Bonds hit .303 with 37 home runs and 28 stolen bases as the Giants barely missed the playoffs. The following year Bonds missed some games due to injuries, and his numbers dropped to .262 with 32 home runs and 16 stolen bases. In 2000 the Giants moved to a new home field, Pacific Bell Park. Bonds liked the shorter fences and responded by hitting a career-high 49 home runs. He improved his average to .306 and finished second in MVP voting. The Giants won their division in 2000 for the second time in four years, but once again they lost in the NLCS.

**Setting the Home Run Record**

The 2001 season was a very special one for Bonds. On April 17 he hit his 500th career home run. "I never dreamed of hitting 500 home runs," he stated. "Everything after that is like icing on the cake." Bonds continued hitting home runs at a remarkable rate over the next few months. As the season progressed, it became clear that he would have a chance to beat the single-season home run record of 70 that had been set by St. Louis Cardinals slugger Mark McGwire three years earlier.

As Bonds made his bid to become baseball's new home run king, some people noticed a slight improvement in the star player's attitude toward

*Bonds hits his record-setting 73rd home run, October 7, 2001.*

*Bonds reacts to his record-setting home run.*

*Bonds runs the bases with a smile, after his 73rd home run.*

teammates, fans, and reporters. He seemed more willing to sign auto-graphs and more patient with the media. "He's made an effort," said Giants Manager Dusty Baker. "Sometimes Barry is tough to deal with, but most of the time he's a gentleman." "I'm just making myself a little bit more accessible to the public, as well as the media," Bonds noted. "I haven't in the past, and it has affected me."

> "There wasn't an amount of money that was going to make me leave San Francisco, to be honest with you," Bonds said after signing a new contract with the Giants. "To retire in a San Francisco Giant uniform . . . that's what I've always wanted to do my whole, entire life. Everyone knows my childhood idol is Willie Mays, and this is the greatest honor and perfect dream for me."

Bonds tied McGwire's record in early October against pitcher Wilfredo Rodriguez of the Houston Astros. "Everything is perfect in that one particular second," he said of his home-run swing. "It's in slow motion. You don't hear anything, you don't even feel it hit your bat. That's the zone." Bonds broke the record a week later against pitcher Chan Ho Park of the Los Angeles Dodgers, then added home run number 72 against Park later the same night. Bonds hit another home run on the final day of the 2001 season to raise the new record to 73. He also set a new major league record for slugging average at .863, breaking a mark that had been held by the great Babe Ruth for 81 years. When the season ended, Bonds became the first player in major league history to win a fourth MVP award.

Following his amazing 2001 season, Bonds signed a five-year, $90 million contract to play out the remainder of his career with the Giants. "There wasn't an amount of money that was going to make me leave San Francisco, to be honest with you," he said afterward. "To retire in a San Francisco Giant uniform . . . that's what I've always wanted to do my whole, entire life. Everyone knows my childhood idol is Willie Mays, and this is the greatest honor and perfect dream for me."

## Making It to the World Series

Many people doubted that Bonds could ever top his outstanding achievements of the 2001 season. Yet the 38-year-old superstar managed to do so the following year. He claimed his first National League batting title with an amazing .370 average. He also set new league records with 198 walks and a .582 on-base percentage. In addition, Bonds hit 46 home runs and tallied 110 RBIs. In August he hit his 600th career home run, placing him fourth on the all-time list for career homers, behind only Hank Aaron, Babe Ruth, and Willie Mays. At the end of the season, Bonds was the unanimous choice as the 2002 National League MVP. He thus became the first five-time MVP, as well as the first player to win the award consecutively two different times.

Making the 2002 season even more special for Bonds was the fact that the Giants reached the World Series by defeating the St. Louis Cardinals in the NLCS. For a while it appeared as if Bonds would finally achieve his dream of a World Series championship. The Giants took a 3-2 lead over the Anaheim Angels in the seven-game series. As Game 6 got underway, they jumped out to a 5-0 lead. They held the lead through the seventh inning and found themselves just seven outs away from the world title. Champagne was placed on ice in the Giants' clubhouse in anticipation of a team celebration. But then the Angels started a rally that led to one of the most remarkable comebacks in World Series history. They chipped away at the Giants' lead and ended up winning the game 6-5 and tying the series 3-3. The Angels then won the deciding game by a score of 4-1.

Unlike his previous playoff performances, Bonds had an outstanding series. He batted an amazing .471 with 4 home runs and 6 RBIs. He also drew a record 13 walks — 7 of them intentional — which helped him to reach base an incredible 21 out of 30 times he was at the plate. Unfortunately, the rest of the Giants only managed to hit a combined .266 for the series. "I don't think it's my last chance," Bonds said after the disappointing World Series loss. "You want the end to be different. What can you do about it? They outplayed us and they deserve it."

When the 2002 season ended, Bonds had 613 career home runs. Some observers predict that he will break Hank Aaron's all-time record of 755 career homers by the time he retires. In addition, Bonds needs only 7 more stolen bases to become the only player ever to achieve over 500 home runs and 500 steals in his career. Despite his individual accomplishments, however, Bonds says that his career will not be complete without a World Series championship. "You hear them say that Barry Bonds is one of the best players in the game today, but I'll never be in the elite category until I win [the World Series]. I have the God-given ability to be a contender, to be a big piece of the puzzle, but so far that's all I have," he noted. "Every year I go through a long season and I get close to a championship, and

*Bonds hits a home run against the Anaheim Angels during game one of the World Series, October 19, 2002.*

every year I go home disappointed. . . . I like putting up good numbers. But if I never reach another milestone, and the Giants finally win a World Series, that's all I could ask for. I'd be complete."

## A Future Member of the Hall of Fame

Bonds is widely considered to be the best all-around player in professional baseball today. His name is often mentioned among the all-time greats, and he will certainly go into the Hall of Fame. He has posted a career batting average of .295 and a career slugging average of .595. His career statistics also include 1,652 RBIs, 1,830 runs scored, and 1,922 walks. Some experts have attributed Bonds's success to his unusual batting style, in which he chokes up on the handle of the bat farther than most professional players. "I started choking up when I was a kid. My dad gave me bats that were too big for me," he recalled. "We had to choke up so we wouldn't fall down [when we swung]." Bonds also possesses some of the quickest hands in the game. The speed of his swing allows him to wait a split second longer than other hitters before swinging at a pitch.

Bonds is known as a keen observer of the game of baseball. He often notices small quirks that clue him into a pitcher's intentions. But he annoys some of his teammates by refusing to share his observations with them. "If you're the star, you're supposed to go out of your way for everybody else," he said. "But I could tell a guy things that I know, and the following year he might be on a team I was talking about, and now he's telling his guys what my tendencies are or what I might do. How smart would that be? Hey man, I've gotta keep my edge."

Despite the slight improvement in his attitude that has taken place in recent years, Bonds still has a reputation as a moody, arrogant, and sometimes difficult player. He remains relatively unpopular among his teammates, who tend to resent some of the special treatment he receives. For example, Bonds never shows up for the annual team picture, refuses to stretch on the field with the team before games, has his own staff to handle his publicity and prepare his meals, and gets his own hotel suite on road trips while the other players share rooms. In the Giants' clubhouse, Bonds sits alone on one side with a fancy leather massage chair and big-screen TV, while his teammates hang out together and play cards on the other side. Bonds claims that he does not need to be popular among his teammates in order to contribute to the team. "The only criticism that really bothers me is when they say I'm not a team player," he stated. "Excuse me? I'm sorry, but that's the one that's not true. Because let me tell you something: You hit .300 every season, knock in a hundred runs, score a hundred runs, hit 30 home runs, you're every inch a team player."

> *"If you're the star, you're supposed to go out of your way for everybody else. But I could tell a guy things that I know, and the following year he might be on a team I was talking about, and now he's telling his guys what my tendencies are or what I might do. How smart would that be? Hey man, I've gotta keep my edge."*

Bonds also continues to have a prickly relationship with the media. He does not like to analyze his game and wishes that reporters would let his on-field performance speak for itself. "Why talk about things?" he asked. "When you talk about stuff too much, you overkill it. You get your glory when the people are happy. That's the glory of it all—when your team wins, you got that big hit, made that big play. That says enough. Why talk about it?"

Finally, Bonds can be less than accommodating with fans. He thinks that people should be satisfied by watching the game of baseball being played at a high level. He does not understand why fans feel entitled to get players' autographs after a game. "Why can't people just enjoy the show? And then let the entertainer go home and get his rest, so he can put on another show?" he stated. "But in baseball, you get to see us, touch us, trade our cards, buy and sell jerseys. To me, that dilutes the excitement. Autograph seekers! When I go to a movie, after the final credits roll, I get up and leave. It's the end! But I'm supposed to stand out there for three hours and then sign autographs? If fans pay $10 to see Batman, they don't expect to get Jack Nicholson's autograph."

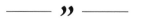

> *Bonds does not understand why fans feel entitled to get players' autographs after a game. "Why can't people just enjoy the show? And then let the entertainer go home and get his rest, so he can put on another show? But in baseball, you get to see us, touch us, trade our cards, buy and sell jerseys. To me, that dilutes the excitement. Autograph seekers! When I go to a movie, after the final credits roll, I get up and leave. It's the end! But I'm supposed to stand out there for three hours and then sign autographs? If fans pay $10 to see Batman, they don't expect to get Jack Nicholson's autograph."*

## HOME AND FAMILY

Bonds has been married twice. He married Susann (known as Sun) Branco on February 6, 1988. They had a son, Nikolai, and a daughter, Shikari, before they divorced in 1994. Bonds married his longtime friend Elizabeth Watson on January 10, 1998. They have a daughter, Aisha Lynn. Bonds lives with his second wife and his three children in a three-story, 12,500-square-foot mansion in Los Altos Hills, California.

Since he remarried, Bonds has made an effort to become more involved in his children's lives. "Before, I just wanted to get to the field. That was my life," he admitted. "Now, I'm like a human carpool. I get up in the morning and take my kids to school and pick them up when I'm not at the ballpark. My kids are doing so many things. And I want to be there for them." His son, Nikolai, is a batboy for the Giants and hopes to become a professional baseball player someday.

## HOBBIES AND OTHER INTERESTS

In his spare time, Bonds likes to watch basketball and hockey on television, play golf, practice martial arts, and ride motorcycles. He has worked on behalf of a wide range of charitable causes over the years, including the Adopt-A-Special-Kid program and the Cardiac Arrhythmias Research and Education Foundation. He also urges African-Americans to register as bone marrow donors.

Helping underprivileged children is one of Bonds's favorite causes, and he has given generously to many youth groups. During his many seasons with the Giants, he has purchased 50 tickets to each home game and given them away to children's organizations.

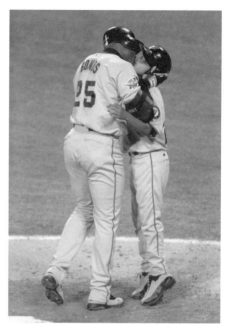

*Bonds kisses his son Nikolai after hitting a home run in game six of the World Series, October 26, 2002.*

The children sit in the leftfield bleachers, and Bonds always tips his hat to them before the game. Bonds also established a scholarship fund for his high school to help disadvantaged kids attend college.

Bonds is also an entrepreneur. He co-founded a company called Digital Interiors that installs high-tech electronic gadgets in people's homes. His own home features several such devices, which allow him to remotely adjust the temperature or fire up the hot tub. Bonds has also recently started doing endorsements for Armour hot dogs, Sega Dreamcast games, Kentucky Fried Chicken, Charles Schwab investments, MasterCard, and Fila.

## HONORS AND AWARDS

College All-America Team (*Sporting News*): 1985
National League Most Valuable Player (Baseball Writers' Association):
    1990, 1992, 1993, 2001, 2002
Major League Player of the Year (*Sporting News*): 1990
National League Player of the Year (*Sporting News*): 1990, 1991
Major League Baseball All-Star Team: 1990, 1992-96
Gold Glove Award: 1990-94, 1996-98

Major League Player of the Year (Associated Press): 1992
Major League Player of the 1990s (*Sporting News*): 2000
Male Athlete of the Year (Associated Press): 2001
Athlete of the Year (*Sports Illustrated for Kids*): 2002

## FURTHER READING

### Books

*Contemporary Black Biography*, Vol. 6, 1994
Harvey, Miles. *Barry Bonds: Baseball's Complete Player*, 1994 (juvenile)
Muskat, Carrie. *Baseball Legends: Barry Bonds*, 1997 (juvenile)
Savage, Jeff. *Barry Bonds: Record Breaker*, 2002 (juvenile)
*Sports Stars*, Series 1-4, 1994-98
Travers, Steven. *Barry Bonds: Baseball's Superman*, 2002
*Who's Who in America*, 2002
*World Book Encyclopedia*, 2002

### Periodicals

*Baseball Digest*, Dec. 2000, p.52
*Current Biography Yearbook*, 1994
*Ebony*, Sep. 1993, p.118; July 2002, p.116
*Esquire*, Aug. 1996, p.46
*Los Angeles Times*, Oct. 7, 2001, Sports sec., p.1
*New York Times*, Oct. 5, 2001, p.D13; Nov. 20, 2001, p.S4; Oct. 24, 2002, p.A1
*New York Times Magazine*, Sep. 1, 2002, p.36
*People*, Oct. 4, 1993, p.101; July 9, 2001, p.63; Oct. 22, 2001, p.73
*San Francisco Chronicle*, Feb. 17, 1997, p.D1; Oct. 6, 2001, p.F1
*Sport*, Apr. 1993, p.60; Oct. 1996, p.16
*Sporting News*, July 12, 1999, p.12
*Sports Illustrated*, June 25, 1990, p.59; May 24, 1993, p.12; June 5, 2000, p.48;
   Aug. 27, 2001, p.102; Oct. 8, 2001, p.38; Oct. 15, 2001, p.46; Aug. 19,
   2002, p.42; Nov. 4, 2002, p.32, 96
*Sports Illustrated for Kids*, Sep. 1, 2001, p.50; Jan. 2002
*Time*, July 2, 2001, p.62; Oct. 28, 2002, p.59
*USA Today*, Aug. 9, 2000, p.C1

### Online Databases

*Biography Resource Center Online*, 2002, articles from *Contemporary Black Biography*, 1994, and *Sports Stars*, 1994-98

## ADDRESS

Barry Bonds
San Francisco Giants
Pacific Bell Park
24 Willie Mays Plaza
San Francisco, CA 94107

## WORLD WIDE WEB SITE

http://sanfrancisco.giants.mlb.com

## Kelly Clarkson 1982-

American Singer
Winner of a Million-Dollar Recording Contract on the
2002 TV Series "American Idol"

### BIRTH

Kelly Clarkson was born on April 24, 1982, in Burleson,
Texas—a town with a population of 27,000 located about 10
miles south of Fort Worth. Her parents, Steve Clarkson and
Jeanne Taylor, separated when she was six years old and eventually divorced. Kelly lived with her mother, a first-grade

teacher, and her stepfather, Jimmy Taylor, a contractor. She has an older sister, Alyssa, an older brother, Jason, and five step-siblings.

## YOUTH

Clarkson was an outgoing and fun-loving child who enjoyed performing from an early age. She often entertained her family by singing songs from Walt Disney musicals, like *Beauty and the Beast* and *The Little Mermaid*, in the living room of their middle-class home. Clarkson also had a kind heart and often tried to help others. As a teenager, she once gave the last five dollars in her wallet to a homeless person, then almost ran out of gas on her way home.

Jeanne Taylor recalled that her daughter had only one major fault growing up. "[Kelly] was easy to raise, except for having to get her up in the morning to go to school," she noted. "When they say she sometimes went [to school] in her pajamas, they mean it. The alarm clock would be blasting right beside her head, and she didn't hear a thing. The house could have fallen apart and she'd still be sleeping."

> "I was going to be in band, and Ms. Glenn, my seventh-grade choir teacher, heard me sing in the hallway and was like, 'Why aren't you in choir?' So I got in and realized I had a talent there."

## EDUCATION

Clarkson attended the public schools in Burleson. She was a good student who impressed her teachers with her energy and willingness to work hard. One of her junior high teachers, Cindy Glenn, convinced her to join the school choir. "I was going to be in band, and Ms. Glenn, my seventh-grade choir teacher, heard me sing in the hallway and was like, 'Why aren't you in choir?'" Clarkson remembered. "So I got in and realized I had a talent there." Before long Clarkson began dreaming of making a career as a professional singer. "My first solo was 'Vision of Love' by Mariah Carey in seventh grade and afterward I told my mom that I thought I might do this for my career," she recalled.

As a student at Burleson High School, Clarkson played on the volleyball team and was a member of the school choir, which performed overseas. She also took part in several school musicals, playing the female lead in a production of *Brigadoon* during her senior year. "Already then Kelly could do any and all musical styles," said Burleson High choir director Philip Glenn. Clarkson graduated from high school in the spring of 2000.

## CAREER HIGHLIGHTS

### Trying to Launch a Singing Career

After graduating from high school, Clarkson recorded demo tapes in hopes of being discovered as a singer. In the meantime, she accepted a series of odd jobs in Burleson. She worked as a cocktail waitress at a comedy club, as a clerk at a bookstore and a pharmacy, as a ticket seller at a movie theater, and as a telemarketer. In 2001 she moved with a friend to Los Angeles, California, in hopes of breaking into show business. During her time in Los Angeles, she appeared as an extra on the TV series "Sabrina, the Teenage Witch" and recorded a few demo tapes for the well-known songwriter Gerry Goffin. But then Clarkson ran into a string of bad luck that made her question her decision to move to California. First Goffin became ill, then her apartment burned down, then her friend decided to leave Los Angeles. Clarkson took the series of events as a sign that she should return home to Texas.

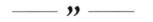

*"Throughout the whole competition, I wasn't looking to win; I was looking for exposure. I'm just an 'average girl,' so I never expect the top. I never look that far in advance."*

Although Clarkson was discouraged when she got back to Burleson, she remained determined to build a career as a singer. She told her mother, "I have to sing, I don't know what else to do." In the meantime, she got a job as a promotional worker for an energy drink. A few days after Clarkson returned from California, she went to visit one of her friends, Jessica Brake. Brake's mother showed the girls an Internet site about an upcoming TV series called "American Idol: The Search for a Superstar." The show—which was based on a popular British show called "Pop Idol"—was supposed to showcase young, unknown singers. On each episode, the singers would perform and then receive comments from a panel of judges. Once the episode ended, TV viewers would have two hours to call in and register their votes for the night's best performer. One singer would be eliminated from the show each week, and the final contestant would win a million-dollar recording contract.

Clarkson learned that auditions for "American Idol" would be held in seven U.S. cities, including nearby Dallas, Texas. Her friend immediately began trying to convince her to attend the Dallas audition. When Clarkson expressed doubts, Brake filled out the online application form for her.

*Clarkson with Guarini.*

Clarkson became more excited as the auditions approached. In fact, she was so worried about sleeping through her audition that she stayed up the whole night before. Across the country, more than 10,000 people between the ages of 16 and 24 tried out to appear on "American Idol." Judges held a series of callbacks to narrow the field to 30 contestants, who were invited to attend tryouts in Hollywood, California. These tryouts reduced the field to ten finalists who would compete on the air. Clarkson performed well at each stage and was selected to appear on "American Idol" as one of the ten finalists.

### Appearing on "American Idol"

Clarkson and the other nine singers were asked to move to California for three months of filming. They all lived together in a 13-bedroom, 8-bathroom estate that featured a pool, hot tub, steam room, big-screen TV, workout equipment, and a chef. But the contestants had very little time to enjoy the luxurious house. Their days were packed with rehearsals, voice coaching, wardrobe selection, and promotional appearances. Clarkson claims that she often survived on three to four hours of sleep per night, and even admitted that "there are days I just don't shower." Despite the hectic schedule and the pressure of the show, however, all the contestants got along very well. "Of course, there are going to be ups and downs with people because of the stress, but nobody got in fights," Clarkson recalled. "We were all too busy. Nobody believes us, but we were literally too busy to have any kind of conflict."

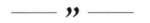

*"I just try to be as real as I can be—the kind of person who doesn't really care if she is caught without makeup, not some ultra-professional musician who is only 'on' when in front of the camera."*

"American Idol" made its premier on the Fox television network on June 11, 2002. Given the number of finalists, Clarkson did not perform in the first episode. The first time viewers got to hear her powerful voice was two weeks later, when she sang "Respect" by Aretha Franklin. "I wasn't on the first two shows and I thought I would have to come out with a big song," she remembered. "I had sung 'Respect' karaoke with friends. I feel that song and I love that song. It's upbeat, it's got soul, it shows your range. It's a show stopper, the song itself." Clarkson received mostly positive comments from the three judges—singer Paula Abdul, record producer Randy Jackson, and British music executive Simon Cowell. She also earned enough votes from viewers to remain on the show.

As the weeks passed, Clarkson turned in consistently strong performances that showcased the power and range of her voice. "I know my voice and what I can do," she explained. "I just rehearse and pray to God that He won't let me screw up on national television." Clarkson also appeared calm on stage and impressed both the judges and the viewers with her sweet, friendly nature. "I just try to be as real as I can be—the kind of person who doesn't really care if she is caught without makeup, not some ultra-professional musician who is only 'on' when in front of the camera,"

she noted. Clarkson also stood out from the other contestants because she wore sophisticated evening attire rather than sexy, belly-baring outfits when she performed. By mid-August, Clarkson had advanced to the final four contestants, along with Justin Guarini, Nikki McKibbin, and Tamyra Gray. She expressed nothing but fondness and admiration for her fellow contestants. "It's not a competition between the contestants," she stated. "It's me competing with myself."

Gray was voted off the show the following week, which shocked many viewers who believed she had the strongest voice in the competition. McKibbin was voted off next, leaving only Clarkson and Guarini to compete for the million-dollar prize. Although the judges and most viewers acknowledged that Clarkson was the better singer, the curly-haired Guarini had good stage presence and a huge fan base among young women, which placed the final vote in doubt. On the second-to-last episode of

*Clarkson poses backstage after winning in the final episode of "American Idol," September 5, 2002.*

"American Idol," Clarkson and Guarini performed the same songs back-to-back. Afterward the three judges, including the notoriously nasty Cowell, praised her performance and recommended that viewers select her as the winner.

## Winning the Viewers' Hearts

Votes were tallied immediately after the show ended, and the winner was announced at the end of a two-hour special episode the following night, September 4. Shortly before the results were announced, Clarkson and Guarini sang a duet of "It Takes Two," which confirmed the fact that Clarkson's voice was much stronger than that of her rival. Finally, the show's hosts announced that Clarkson had defeated Guarini with 58 percent of the viewer vote to become the first American Idol and win the million-dollar recording contract. More than 15 million people had called in to express their opinions. Clarkson was surprised when she learned she had won. "Throughout the whole competition, I wasn't looking to win; I was looking for exposure," she explained. "I'm just an 'average girl,' so I never expect the top. I never look that far in advance."

Guarini was gracious in defeat, declaring that "No one deserves it more than this woman right here." "He is so sweet," Clarkson responded. "He is just the greatest. He didn't have to say what he said. He's a great guy inside and out. I know that he will probably outsell all of us. He's such a cutie and such a great writer." Several of the other finalists also expressed their agreement with the result of the final vote. "Kelly is phenomenal," said McKibbin. "Starting with that incredible voice. She has obviously been the crowd favorite and she just deserves every stitch of everything she is receiving." Shortly after learning that she had won, Clarkson was asked to sing "A Moment Like This," a song written especially for the "American Idol" winner. She struggled to get through the song while fighting back tears of happiness. The other finalists joined in to help her with the last few minutes of the finale.

Clarkson's life was a whirlwind in the weeks following the "American Idol" final vote. She appeared on countless TV talk shows and magazine covers, filmed music videos and a VH-1 documentary about her life, and launched a 28-city concert tour with the other finalists. Throughout all of the publicity, Clarkson was often asked whether the obviously close relationship between her and Guarini had turned romantic. She insisted that they were just friends and described her heartthrob fellow finalist as "like a broth-

*"Being on stage in front of millions is the biggest rush for me. It's like I'm kind of nervous at first, but once I get out there I never want to leave the stage!"*

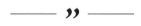

er." "Everyone always says there's something between me and Justin, but we get along so well because we are both so focused," she explained. "Neither of us wants to start a relationship knowing we don't have the time to sleep let alone have a boyfriend."

Fans of "American Idol" also wanted to hear Clarkson's opinion of the show's acid-tongued judge, Simon Cowell. "He is a great guy off camera, funny as anything," she revealed. "But, I mean, on the show, and with his business in general, he's very serious and he doesn't want to work with people he doesn't think can handle the pressure or he doesn't think are good enough. I mean he's going to be honest with you business-wise but he's a great guy in general when you're not on camera or talking about business." Still, Clarkson admitted that her favorite judge was Randy Jackson. "He's the one who's been on every side of the whole equation for making an album," she noted. Clarkson added that the judges' comments were not difficult for her to take because "it's three people's opinion. There are a lot more people in the industry. Simon is not a fan of Britney Spears, and look how well she is doing."

## Turning TV Success into a Recording Career

Although Clarkson received a great deal of attention as the winner of "American Idol," some people wondered whether she would be able to turn it into a successful recording career. She got off to a good start with her first single. "A Moment Like This"/ "Before Your Love" hit No. 1 on the *Billboard* Top 100 charts, selling 236,000 copies in a single week. Clarkson also contributed four songs, including "Respect" and "You Make Me Feel Like a Natural Woman" as well as the two songs from her single, to the *American Idol: Greatest Moments* collection. This album featured two songs from Guarini and one song from each of the other finalists. In addition, all ten finalists sang together on the song "California Dreamin.'"

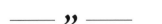

> "The one thing I love about this show is our versatility, and I hope to do that on my album. I want to do a kind of rock meets soul, and I hope people are open to that since I've done that on the show. I'm all about my sound and my style. That's important for me to stand up to. I came out on the show being myself and doing what I like, and people voted for me. So I already have a fan base based on what I like and what I do."

Clarkson also began working on her solo album, which was scheduled for release in early 2003. Her record label recruited several well-known songwriters to provide material for it, and Clarkson hoped to add some of her own compositions. "The one thing I love about this show is our versatility, and I hope to do that on my album. I want to do a kind of rock meets soul, and I hope people are open to that since I've done that on the show," she noted. "I'm all about my sound and my style. That's important for me to stand up to. I came out on the show being myself and doing what I like, and people voted for me. So I already have a fan base based on what I like and what I do."

But some music industry insiders worried that Clarkson could become a "one-hit wonder" once the popularity of *American Idol* wore off. They criticized the songs that were included on her single and warned that she needed better material if her album was to be a success. "Celine Dion or

Mariah Carey wouldn't cross the street to spit on those songs. And that's who Kelly is competing against now — it's not just Justin anymore," said *Rolling Stone* music editor Joe Levy. "People voted for Kelly because she had a sweetness and a vulnerability in addition to astounding ability. They've got to give her songs that communicate something about her personality. Otherwise, she might as well be queen of the Thanksgiving Day parade rather than a pop star."

Clarkson experienced the downside of her newfound fame just a few days after her "American Idol" victory, when she was contacted by Champions of Hope, a national youth organization. The youth group invited her to sing the national anthem at the Lincoln Memorial in Washington, D.C., as part of a ceremony honoring the anniversary of the terrorist attacks of September 11, 2001. But many people criticized the group's choice. They claimed that Clarkson had only come to public attention through "reality

TV." They argued that allowing her to sing would be inappropriate because it would promote "American Idol" during a day of mourning. Upon learning of the controversy, Clarkson expressed some reservations about singing in Washington. "If I do it, I will get criticized, and if I don't do it and pull out of it, I'll also get criticized," she said. "It's a lose-lose situation." With the support of her management company, however, Clarkson did appear at the event.

Despite the hectic schedule and constant attention, Clarkson thoroughly enjoyed her experience on "American Idol." "Being on stage in front of millions is the biggest rush for me," she explained. "It's like I'm kind of nervous at first, but once I get out there I never want to leave the stage!" She also offered the following advice for future contestants: "Be confident. Do not show fear. That's the one thing Simon and Randy will get you for. They know a performer must be fearless. If you feel it, don't show it. Also take what's unique about you and go with it."

*Clarkson offers the following advice for future contestants: "Be confident. Do not show fear. That's the one thing Simon and Randy will get you for. They know a performer must be fearless. If you feel it, don't show it. Also take what's unique about you and go with it."*

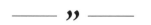

## HOME AND FAMILY

Clarkson is not married and says she has no time for dating. She loves her home state and her fellow Texans, and she plans to remain there even if she becomes a pop star. "I'm living in Texas. I don't care how many times I have to fly," she stated. "I've been everywhere—New York and LA—and it's just a different feel when you go to Texas. . . . Everyone knows each other, so if you meet one person, you'll meet the whole town through them. We're just cool."

Clarkson remains close to her family. Her father, mother, stepfather, brother, and sister were all part of the studio audience for the final episodes of "American Idol." "My parents have been so supportive and kept me grounded," she noted. "I come from a Godly family and I know that helps."

## HOBBIES AND OTHER INTERESTS

In her spare time, Clarkson loves watching movies. She has written a few film scripts and says she might try acting someday. She also wants to learn to play guitar. She plans to use some of her "American Idol" winnings to buy a 2003 Corvette for her friend Jessica Brake, who convinced her to audition for the show.

## FURTHER READING

### Periodicals

*Austin American Statesman,* Sep. 3, 2002, p.E1

*Dallas Morning News,* July 2, 2002, p.A19; Aug. 20, 2002, p.C1; Aug. 29, 2002, p.A33; Sep. 4, 2002, pp.A1, A25; Sep. 5, 2002, p.A15

*Fort Worth Star-Telegram,* July 24, 2002, Life and Arts sec., p.1; Sep. 5, 2002, News sec., p.1; Sep. 10, 2002, Metro sec., p.2; Sep. 28, 2002, Metro sec., p.1

*Houston Chronicle,* Sep. 9, 2002, p.3

*Los Angeles Times,* Sep. 5, 2002, p.A15; Sep. 23, 2002, p.F14

*New York Post,* Sep. 5, 2002, p.7; Sep. 6, 2002, p.111; Sep. 7, 2002, p.53

*New York Times,* Sep. 8, 2002, p.L1

*People,* Sep. 9, 2002, p.52

*Tampa Tribune,* Sep. 6, 2002, p.2

*TV Guide,* July 13, 2002, p.10; Sep. 21, 2002, p.40

*Us,* Sep. 23, 2002, p.44

*USA Today,* Aug. 29, 2002, p.D3; Sep. 5, 2002, p.D1; Sep. 26, 2002, p.D1

*Washington Post,* Sep. 5, 2002, p.C1

*YM,* Nov. 2002, p.86

## ADDRESS

Kelly Clarkson
RCA Records
1540 Broadway
New York, NY 10036

## WORLD WIDE WEB SITES

http://idolonfox.com
http://www.rcarecords.com
http://www.rollingstone.com/artists/bio.asp?oid=2044862&cf=2044862

## Vin Diesel 1967-

American Actor
Star of the Hit Action Movies *The Fast and the Furious*
and *XXX*

### BIRTH

Vin Diesel was born on July 18, 1967, in New York City. His
name was originally Mark Vincent, but he changed it when he
was in his late teens. Vin was raised by his mother, Delora, an
astrologer and psychologist, and his stepfather, Irving, an
actor and drama teacher. He never knew his biological father
and claims that he still has "no overwhelming desire to meet

him." Vin has a non-identical twin brother, film editor Paul Vincent, as well as two younger step-siblings.

## YOUTH

Diesel grew up in the Manhattan section of New York City. His family lived in a small apartment in Westbeth, a government-funded housing complex in trendy Greenwich Village that was home to many actors, artists, and musicians. Diesel enjoyed exploring the city as a boy. "I had this magical childhood," he remembered. "In the winter, I remember my father pulling my brother and me around Washington Square Park in a cheap red plastic sled. In the summer, my mother would take us to the fountain at the park, and we'd swim in it."

Perhaps due to the influence of his stepfather, Diesel always wanted to be an actor. "Acting is the only thing I ever knew that I wanted to do. People are designed differently and I think I was designed in a way that I needed to perform and work out my things in front of the camera," he noted. "I was a huge fan of *Mad Max, The Terminator,* and *Conan the Barbarian* growing up. Whenever I was asked what I wanted to do when I grew up, I always said, 'Actor.' But if that was too implausible and I needed something to fall back on, my second choice would always be 'Superhero.'"

> "
>
> *"I had this magical childhood. In the winter, I remember my father pulling my brother and me around Washington Square Park in a cheap red plastic sled. In the summer, my mother would take us to the fountain at the park, and we'd swim in it."*
>
> "

Diesel's interest in performing was apparent from an early age. For example, he went to the circus with his family when he was three years old. Once the show ended and all the animals and clowns had left the ring, Diesel tried to climb in. When his mother grabbed him and asked what he was doing, the little boy replied, "Mommy, I'm ready to do *my* show." At the age of five, Diesel was cast in a Westbeth children's production of *Cinderella.* He played a horse, while his twin brother got the role of Prince Charming. But Paul suffered from stage fright and was too scared to go onstage. Diesel ended up covering for him and becoming the star of the show.

Diesel joined a local theater company at the age of seven, after he and some of his neighborhood friends broke into the building where the group performed. "We were terrorizing the neighborhood, a few of us, and we went into this theater," he recalled. "We went in and we were vandalizing the theater, playing around in the mezzanine, and this woman comes out in the spotlight, this heavyset woman who summons us. I thought she was going to get us in trouble and call the cops on us. She said, 'If you guys want to play here, come every day at four o'clock. Know your lines.' That was the first time I was ever able to make a whole audience laugh without getting sent to the dean's office."

————— " —————

*"I am truly multicultural. I'm neither black nor white. People like to put each other in boxes because it allows them to categorize, create labels, and stereotype. In the neighborhood where I grew up, most of the kids I knew were multiracial. I had to deal with a lot of [stuff] growing up because I'm multicultural, and there were no multicultural icons or role models. It was a struggle to define myself as a person up against other people's expectations."*

————— " —————

Diesel's racial heritage is a bit ambiguous. Many sources say his background includes African-American, Italian-American, and several other groups, although Diesel has avoided clarifying this. He does say that throughout his childhood, he struggled to come to terms with his heritage. The situation was difficult because he did not know his biological father, and his stepfather was black. As a result, Diesel always identified with many ethnic groups and resisted being linked with any one group. "I am truly multicultural. I'm neither black nor white," he stated. "People like to put each other in boxes because it allows them to categorize, create labels, and stereotype. In the neighborhood where I grew up, most of the kids I knew were multiracial. I had to deal with a lot of [stuff] growing up because I'm multicultural, and there were no multicultural icons or role models. It was a struggle to define myself as a person up against other people's expectations."

## EDUCATION

Diesel's parents were educated people who emphasized the importance of learning. Diesel received his education at the prestigious Anglo-American International School in New York City. It was a private school in which half of the students came from foreign countries. After earning his high school diploma, Diesel studied acting at the Theater for the New City and English at Hunter College.

## CAREER HIGHLIGHTS

### Struggling to Make It as an Actor

Committed to building a career as an actor, Diesel performed in the repertory theater run by his father, then started appearing in off-off-Broadway plays. When he was 17, the muscular young man started working as a bouncer at some of New York City's trendiest nightclubs. Many of his fellow bouncers were known by nicknames, so he started calling himself Vin Diesel during this time. "I started bouncing because you need to have your days free to go and audition, rehearse, to be involved in theatrical productions," he explained. "The best job in the world was one that started at ten and ended at four in the morning. It was also a great job for someone at college. I don't think I was ever servile enough to be a waiter. I was always attracted to that nocturnal world."

Diesel ended up working as a bouncer for nine years while he struggled to make it as an actor. He eventually noticed that the tough-guy image he cultivated as a bouncer was hurting his chances at auditions. "What happened was I was going up for acting jobs and saying, 'Hi, my name is Vin Diesel,' and unwittingly reinforcing it with this giant monster standing behind me that I thought I'd left at work," he noted. "Even when I would go on auditions, and I had to be as amiable as possible, I still had this edge, this threatening physical presence. And I know that isn't who I really am."

In the early 1990s, Diesel took his life savings and some money borrowed from friends and moved to Hollywood, in California. He hoped that his experience on the New York stage would help him land roles in movies. After failing to find work for a year, however, he was forced to return to New York. At this point, he moved back in with his parents and spent his time watching classic movies on video. One day his mother gave him a book about filmmaking called *Feature Films at Used Car Prices*. Since Diesel was frustrated at his inability to find acting jobs, she suggested that he try making a movie of his own.

Diesel was captivated with the idea of shooting his own film. He wrote a screenplay about his own struggles to get discovered as an actor. Then he turned the screenplay into a short film, which he directed, produced, and starred in. The film, called *Multi-Facial*, was shot in two days for a budget of $3,000. It tells the story of a mixed-race aspiring actor who will play a character of any race in order to get a part. Diesel's film made its debut at the Anthology Film Archives in Manhattan in front of 200 people. In 1995 it was screened at the prestigious Cannes Film Festival in France, where it came to the attention of several high-profile filmmakers. "That night changed my life completely," Diesel remembered. "I still went through a few more years of sleeping on couches and struggling and taking odd jobs outside film. But I knew my life had changed."

The success of *Multi-Facial* gave Diesel the confidence to move back to Hollywood the following year. He took a job as a telemarketer in order to raise enough money to make a feature-length film. Once again acting as writer, director, producer, and star, Diesel created *Strays,* a film about a group of lowlife buddies living on New York's Lower East Side. Diesel's character, Rick, realizes that his friends are preventing him from reaching his goals when he meets Heather (played by Suzanne Lanza). Rick ends up feeling torn between his macho street image and the kind, sensitive side he shows to Heather. *Strays* was screened at the respected Sundance Film Festival in Utah in 1997, but it did not sell as well as Diesel had hoped.

> *"I hated that I was the first to die,"Diesel said about his role in* **Saving Private Ryan.** *"But, looking back, it made sense for [Spielberg] to kill the most formidable character first because you got a sense of the dangers that were present at war. The producer said afterwards that it was fortunate that I died first because everyone was now in restless anticipation of what I would do next as they didn't get enough of me the first time."*

**Being Discovered**

Although Diesel's efforts as a film-maker did not earn much money, they did provide him with valuable exposure that led to important career opportunities. After seeing *Multi-Facial,* the famous director Steven Spielberg created a part for Diesel in his 1998 World War II movie *Saving Private Ryan.* Diesel played Private Adrian Caparzo, a tough-talking soldier with a soft heart. Caparzo ends up being the first member of the unit to be killed. He is shot by a German sniper as he tries to save the life of a French girl. "I hated that I was the first to die," Diesel admitted. "But, looking back, it made sense for [Spielberg] to kill the most formidable character first because you got a sense of the dangers that were present at war. The producer said afterwards that it was fortunate that I died first because everyone was now in restless anticipation of what I would do next as they didn't get enough of me the first time."

*Saving Private Ryan* went on to become a critical and audience hit, winning five Academy Awards. Thanks to his prominent role in Spielberg's picture,

Diesel soon had his choice of acting roles. "That was a huge turning point because it introduced me, of course, to Hollywood," he recalled. "There's something about being *Saving Private Ryan*'s Vin Diesel as opposed to the director of *Strays* and the director of *Multi-Facial*, an independent film-maker, that carries some validation, which is a huge blessing."

In 1999 Diesel provided his deep, gravelly voice to the title character in the animated film *The Iron Giant.* Based on a 1968 children's book by Ted Hughes, the movie tells the story of a young boy named Hogarth who meets a 50-foot-tall, metal-eating robot. At first Hogarth is frightened by the Iron Giant, but he still saves the creature when it becomes entangled in power lines. Hogarth takes the robot to live at a nearby scrap-metal yard, and the pair forge an unlikely friendship. But when local residents discover the Iron Giant, they call in government agents to deal with the creature, which they view as a threat. Diesel enjoyed giving voice to such a memorable animated character. "*Iron Giant* was one of the most amazing experiences," he noted. "It's such a positive film. We know that *Iron Giant* will be around forever, and it feels good to be associated with that, so loveable a character."

## Getting His First Leading Roles

In 2000 Diesel played major roles in two very different movies that happened to open at the same time. First he played Richard Riddick in the low-budget science-fiction thriller *Pitch Black*. Riddick has been convicted of murder and is being taken to prison on a space transport when the ship crash lands on a desolate planet. The crash allows Riddick to escape from the lawman who is responsible for him. At first the crew of the ship fear that Riddick will come after them. But in that hostile environment, the group comes together to fight the aliens and Riddick emerges as an unlikely leader and hero.

Diesel received positive reviews for his performance, and *Pitch Black* became a sort of cult classic. Marc Bernardin of *Entertainment Weekly* called the movie "intense and intelligent, unpredictable and inevitable." Diesel liked the Riddick character and the message that his transformation gave to the audience. "The film describes him as this convicted killer, but doesn't give any explanation or justification for it," he explained. "We find out later that maybe he was misrepresented. Maybe we prejudged him. Maybe we just critiqued him and measured him by what we heard. The Riddick character represents anybody who's been ruled out, given up on, or prejudged."

Although Diesel appreciated his character, he did not enjoy the experience of filming *Pitch Black* in the Australian desert. "I'm an ignorant guy from New York. You say desert, I think hot. It was freezing," he remembered. "The crew were standing around with ear muffs on, and I was in a tank top with the wardrobe lady spraying water on me to look like sweat." Adding to his discomfort were the hard plastic contact lenses he had to wear to make his eyes look yellow. He compared wearing the lenses to putting hubcaps into his eyes. In fact, the lenses became stuck in his eyes during the first day of filming, and the director had to fly an eye doctor to the remote set to help Diesel remove them. "Between [the contacts] and the weather I needed absolutely no motivation to play homicidal," he admitted.

Diesel's second movie of 2000 was *Boiler Room*, a film about the pressure-filled world of stockbrokers that co-starred Ben Affleck and Giovanni Ribisi. Diesel played Chris Varick, a fast-talking, Italian-American stockbroker who makes a fortune by selling questionable investments to unsuspecting clients over the phone. Diesel enjoyed the fact that his character in *Boiler Room* was so different from his character in *Pitch Black*. The two movies opened at the same time, which allowed Diesel to demonstrate the range of his acting talents. "I picked this because it was a different kind of part," he said of *Boiler Room*. "I was in a suit and a tie the whole time, and there's something cool about that. There's something that adds to my filmography, the fact that this character in *Boiler Room* has nothing to do with this physically overbearing character in *Pitch Black*."

*"I picked this because it was a different kind of part," Diesel said of* **Boiler Room**. *"I was in a suit and a tie the whole time, and there's something cool about that. There's something that adds to my filmography, the fact that this character in* **Boiler Room** *has nothing to do with this physically overbearing character in* **Pitch Black**.*"

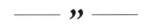

Shortly after Diesel began landing major roles in movies, rumors began spreading around Hollywood that he was difficult to work with. These rumors started after he had a disagreement with director John Frankenheimer on the set of the action-thriller *Reindeer Games*. Diesel claims that upon reading the script, he was unhappy with his character. He says that Frankenheimer agreed to rewrite the role, but failed to follow through on his promise. When Diesel showed up on the set and found the script unchanged, he simply bowed out of the role. "I was inconsequential to the picture and thought I was leaving on good terms, that I did the right thing," he stated. "But Frankenheimer's ego was so bruised, he actually took the time to tell *Premiere* that he fired me. No director in the world would take time out to talk about firing a guy as insignificant as he thought I was."

*Vin Diesel (black car) and Paul Walker (front car) in* The Fast and the Furious.

### The Fast and the Furious

With his unconventional looks and muscular build, Diesel was a natural to play leading roles in action movies. In 2001 he played outlaw street racer Dominic Toretto in the block-buster *The Fast and the Furious.* In the film, Diesel's character is one of the best drivers in Los Angeles and the leader of a crew of rebels. When Toretto's crew is suspected of being involved in a series of high-profile carjackings, an undercover cop infiltrates the street-racing scene. The hot cars and fast action carried *The Fast and the Furious* to the top of the box office charts.

Although his character was a car nut and ace driver, Diesel admits that he did not know much about cars before making the movie. "I'm not that car-oriented, like I couldn't build an engine," he noted. "I grew up in New York City, so I guess I am more familiar with subways." Diesel tried to portray

Toretto as a complex character who has a tough side but is also very giving. "There's something very consistent about Dominic," he explained. "He lives outside of the law but he has his own moral code, which consists of many favorable and admirable attributes. He's honest, he's loyal, and he's a caretaker."

## *XXX*

Diesel stayed with the action-movie genre in 2002, when he starred in the thriller *XXX*. He played Xander Cage, an underground athlete who sells videos of himself performing dangerous and often illegal stunts. Cage is finally arrested when he steals a politician's car, drives it off a bridge, and then parachutes to safety. But this stunt attracts the attention of the National Security Agency (NSA). The government agency decides that Cage's athletic ability—as well as the fact that they consider him expendable—would make him a good secret agent. He undergoes training and is then sent to Europe, where he tries to stop a terrorist group from using biological weapons against the United States. Using the code name XXX, or Triple X, Cage eventually comes to appreciate getting an opportunity to save the world. "At first, this character doesn't care about the state of the world, like a large part of our youth," Diesel noted. "And then he is recruited to save the world. The guy who is least likely to believe in anything learns to believe in something."

Diesel viewed his character as a sort of James Bond spy hero for a new generation. Xander Cage was intended to appeal to an audience that enjoyed the X-Games, body piercing, and industrial rock. "I mean, James Bond wears a suit. I don't know a kid today who wears a suit. So we've come up with a different kind of hero," Diesel explained. "A guy who's proficient at what he does because of all the time he wasted not doing his homework and learning how to do Superman grabs on a motocross instead. The kind of action hero people can relate to today."

*"There's something very consistent about Dominic,"* Diesel said about his character in **The Fast and the Furious.** *"He lives outside of the law but he has his own moral code, which consists of many favorable and admirable attributes. He's honest, he's loyal, and he's a caretaker."*

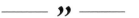

Diesel went through a great deal of training in order to perform the complicated, dangerous stunts that appear in *XXX*. He trained with Navy SEALs, an elite group of highly trained naval officers. Diesel earned how to speed-climb cliffs, ride a snowboard, and jump a motocross bike. Although he did many of his own stunts, the most harrowing feats — like snowboarding down a mountain just ahead of an avalanche — were performed by professional stunt men. "I wanted to push the envelope as much as possible," Diesel said. "But I could not do it without my stunt team. The most amazing things were done by the professionals." The movie's nonstop action, along with its Generation X attitude and humor, helped propel *XXX* to the top of the box office charts in the weeks after its opening.

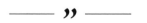

*Diesel viewed his character Xander Cage as a sort of James Bond spy hero for a new generation. "I mean, James Bond wears a suit. I don't know a kid today who wears a suit. So we've come up with a different kind of hero. A guy who's proficient at what he does because of all the time he wasted not doing his homework and learning how to do Superman grabs on a motocross instead. The kind of action hero people can relate to today."*

Following *XXX*, Diesel could be seen in theaters in *Knockaround Guys* (2002). This action film involves a mob family. One of the sons loses a bag of his father's money in a small Montana town, so several tough guys go to find it. But a crooked sheriff beats them to the bag and the cash, which leads to a lot of mayhem as they try to retrieve it. Following on the heels of Diesel's two blockbuster films, *Knockaround Guys* was less successful at the box office.

**Living with Stardom**

The success of Diesel's action films has led to a huge demand for his services. Some of his future projects include *Diablo,* in which he plays a drug enforcement agent who suffers from a mental breakdown; *Doorman,* based on his own script about his days as a bouncer; and sequels to *Pitch Black* (called *Riddick*) and *XXX*. Diesel has been careful to vary his roles so that he will not be pigeonholed as an action hero. "I don't want someone to think that's all I can do and then I can't have a career after 50, which is why I try to speckle my career with choices like *Boiler Room* and *Knockaround Guys,* less explosive-oriented films," he explained.

Some critics claim that part of Diesel's appeal comes from his mixed racial background. They say that his unwillingness to reveal his ethnicity has al-

*Diesel in a scene from XXX.*

lowed various audiences to adopt him as one of their own. Diesel is pleased that he can provide a role model for multicultural youths. "When I was younger there weren't any multicultural heroes. There was no such thing as a person who could list down 10 different nationalities. I feel I've overcome some stuff. What used to be the most restrictive aspect about me attaining my goals is now my ally," he stated. "In the early part of my career nobody knew what to do with me, but now I find I can do so many things because I come from origins that are a little ambiguous. I think I represent a certain future."

Although his imposing physical presence has led Diesel to play many tough characters, he is known for his ability to give those characters a gentler side. "Every character that I have, no matter how menacing he may appear to be, I try to layer it with colors," he noted. "And usually somewhere in that character, you'll find a door to his innocence." This combination of toughness and sensitivity has won Diesel huge numbers of female fans. "I never thought of myself as a sex symbol. It's always kind of weird and it's the one claim that kind of makes me blush," he admitted. "But it's very, very flattering."

Diesel claims that he would still be an actor even if he had never become a star. "The happiness that I derive from acting is a byproduct. It's a coinci-

*Diesel in a scene from* Knockaround Guys.

dence," he stated. "I act because I have to act. I've done it all my life, when the chips were down, I've done it because it's something that I have to do and that's the bottom line." He says that his 20-year struggle to make it as an actor "forced me to have huge respect for the craft. I'll give lines to other actors, I'll cast people who I know will steal scenes from me. It's really about the fact that I could die at any moment and if that's the last film I make, well, it had better be good."

## HOME AND FAMILY

In 2000, Diesel purchased an 1,800-square-foot house with a pool in the Hollywood Hills, which he shares with his dog. "Getting a house was a huge, huge deal because my family always rented," he noted. Diesel, who is single, claims that he has little time for dating, though he has been linked romantically with several actresses and models. He says that he eventually wants to get married and have "a whole bunch of kids."

Diesel remains close to his parents, as well as many old friends from his neighborhood. Speaking about his stepfather, Diesel says that "My father taught me how to be a stand-up man, a man who fights for what he believes in. To me, my father is the pinnacle of what a real man is. In fact, it's hard to live up to him. I think I am fortunate that the people around me are very real. My friends are friends that I've had for many, many years and that's one way to keep your feet on the ground."

## HOBBIES AND OTHER INTERESTS

In his spare time, Diesel enjoys yoga, Playstation, Dungeons and Dragons, classic movies, and Italian cooking.

## FILMS

*Multi-Facial,* 1994
*Strays,* 1997
*Saving Private Ryan,* 1998
*The Iron Giant,* 1999
*Pitch Black,* 2000
*Boiler Room,* 2000
*The Fast and the Furious,* 2001
*XXX,* 2002
*Knockaround Guys,* 2002

## FURTHER READING

### Books

*Contemporary Black Biography,* Vol. 29, 2001

### Periodicals

*Boston Herald,* Feb. 14, 2000, p.31; Aug. 6, 2002, p.37
*Entertainment Weekly,* Aug. 2, 2002, p.24; Aug. 16, 2002, p.43

*"My father taught me how to be a stand-up man, a man who fights for what he believes in. To me, my father is the pinnacle of what a real man is. In fact, it's hard to live up to him. I think I am fortunate that the people around me are very real. My friends are friends that I've had for many, many years and that's one way to keep your feet on the ground."*

*GQ,* Aug. 2002, p.109
*Houston Chronicle,* Aug. 4, 2002, p.10
*Interview,* Feb. 1999, p.40
*Los Angeles Daily News,* June 21, 2001, p.L3; Aug. 9, 2002, p.U6
*Los Angeles Times,* May 28, 2002, Calendar Sec., p.1
*Minneapolis Star-Tribune,* Feb. 19, 2000, p.E4
*Newsweek,* Aug. 5, 2002, p.56
*People,* Aug. 19, 2002, p.87
*Seattle Times,* Feb. 18, 2000, p.F7; Aug. 4, 2002, p.L3
*Time,* Aug. 5, 2002, p.61
*USA Today,* Aug. 7, 2002, p.D1

## Online Articles

http://www.cnn.com/2000/SHOWBIZ/Movies/02/21/vin.diesel/index.html
    (*CNN.com,* "The Drive of Vin Diesel," Feb. 21, 2000)
http://chat.msn.com/msnlive_feature.msnw?id=artist/vindiesel
    (*MSN Celebrity Chats,* "Vin Diesel," June 2001 and Aug. 2002)
http://www.rollingstone.com/news/newsarticle.asp?nid=14127
    (*RollingStone.com,* "Diesel Fuel," July 19, 2001)
http://actionadventure.about.com/library/weekly/2001/aa072801a.htm
    (*About.com,* "You Vin Some, You Lose Some," July 28, 2001)
http://actionadventure.about.com/library/weekly/2002/aa072902.htm
    (*About.com,* "XXX-Rated Interview with Vin Diesel," July 29, 2002)

## Online Databases

*Biography Resource Center Online,* 2001, article from *Contemporary Black Biography,* 2001

## ADDRESS

Vin Diesel
The Firm
9100 Wilshire Boulevard
Beverly Hills, CA 90212

## WORLD WIDE WEB SITE

http://us.imdb.com/Bio?Diesel,+Vin

# Michele Forman 1946-
American High School History Teacher
2001 National Teacher of the Year

## BIRTH

Michele Forman was born in Biloxi, Mississippi, on April 7, 1946.

## YOUTH AND EDUCATION

During Forman's childhood, her family moved from Mississippi to Atlanta, Georgia. She attended school in Atlanta, graduating from Sylvan Hills High School. She then went on to earn a bachelor's degree in history from Brandeis University in Massachusetts in 1967.

A few weeks after graduating from college, Forman joined the Peace Corps. Established in 1961 by President John F. Kennedy, the Peace Corps is a volunteer program run by the United States government that recruits and trains Americans to serve in nations around the world. Many Peace Corps volunteers work on projects that are designed to raise the living standards of people who live in villages, addressing such issues as agriculture, health standards, education, and business development. Forman served two years as a Peace Corps volunteer in Nepal, in south-central Asia. It's home to the Himalayas and to Mount Everest, the highest mountain in the world. In Nepal, Forman taught health classes to young people. "Everything was new—the country, culture, language, subject, and school system—not to mention teaching itself," she recalled. "I learned so much and found enormous rewards in teaching."

After leaving the Peace Corps, Forman returned to the United States. She settled in Vermont in 1970. Over the next decade she served as president of a nursery school, taught at the University of Vermont, and worked as an alcohol and drug education curriculum specialist for the Vermont Department of Education. In 1983 she earned a master's degree in teaching from the University of Vermont.

## CAREER HIGHLIGHTS

### Becoming a Respected High School Teacher

In 1986 Forman found her calling in the field of education. She accepted a position teaching social studies and history at Middlebury Union High School in Middlebury, Vermont. "Most of my career I have taught a range of world and U.S. history offerings and some social studies classes," she explained. "I especially enjoy teaching history because I find it fascinating and essential to all of us in understanding who we are." Forman decided that high school students were the ideal age group for her to teach. "I feel a special affinity for this age group and am fascinated by their intellectual development and creativity," she stated.

Forman developed a strong and supportive relationship with her students. She worked hard to create a classroom environment where her students would feel comfortable. "Making each student feel physically and psychologically safe and comfortable creates a sense of community and enables learning. Only in such an environment are students willing to take intellectual risks," she noted. "Whether it is big pillows in the resource area of the room, student artwork adorning every available space, or plants hanging from the ceiling, the room is above all my students' place much more than mine. In such an atmosphere, trust and respect, as well as collaboration, come naturally and learning is fun." Forman also tried to remove any obstacles to learning for her students. "If they're not feeling well, I make them a cup of peppermint tea," she said. "If they're hungry, I feed them. It can be the simplest thing, but it sends an important message."

Over the years, Forman expanded her role as a teacher to include serving as an advisor for several extracurricular classes and activities. For example, she started a non-credit Arabic language course that met three days per week for 45 minutes before school. To prepare to teach the course, Forman studied Arabic language and culture in a strict immersion program at Middlebury College. She spent two months living in the dormitories and speaking nothing but Arabic. "One of the reasons I chose to learn Arabic was that increasing my students' understanding of the Arab culture through that language could powerfully decrease the stereotypes many of them held of Arabs and Muslims," she explained. "My students' understanding of world history increased because of the new knowledge and resources I brought back to my classroom and, just as importantly, they gained a new understanding of and respect for the Arab world."

*Forman tries to remove any obstacles to learning for her students. "If they're not feeling well, I make them a cup of peppermint tea. If they're hungry, I feed them. It can be the simplest thing, but it sends an important message."*

In 1990 Forman helped a group of students found a new student group, as she explains here. "The Student Coalition on Human Rights came about years ago when we decided that we wanted to celebrate Martin Luther King and his message," she recalled. "And students actually formed it and came together. And they decided that there were many human rights issues that they wanted to learn more about and that they wanted to educate their peers and others about." With Forman as their faculty advisor, the group brought a portion of the AIDS quilt to Middlebury and led local events during the statewide Holocaust Days of Remembrance.

In the past few years, Forman has been working with her students to form a model United Nations program. Model UN, as it's called, is a program in which students act as diplomats from around the world, assuming the roles of the delegates to the United Nations. The goal is to help students gain a broader perspective on contemporary international issues and to develop speech and debate skills. Forman feels that it is important to engage young people in world issues. "They have a lot to say. They have a lot to offer," she said of her students. "And I think we can learn a great deal from their idealism, because they know the world can be a better place and they have the energy and the idealism to work and make it that way. They're creative problem solvers. And they're wonderful to work with." Forman also became involved in professional activities outside of school. For example, she helped write the National World History Standards, headed the College Board History and Social Studies Academic Advisory Committee, helped design her school district's social studies curriculum, and trained numerous student teachers.

———— *"* ————

*"There is little she wouldn't do for her students," said Forman's team-teaching partner, Richard Seubert. "Along with high expectations, she cares for them as human beings first, which helps kids appreciate their potential and set goals that push them to higher levels. She doesn't talk down to them but promotes a dialogue which honors their ideas and celebrates their uniqueness as human beings."*

———— *"* ————

### Named National Teacher of the Year for 2001

Throughout her career, Forman has earned the respect of her students, fellow teachers, and school administrators for her excellence in teaching. Her colleagues have praised her knowledge of the subjects she taught, her use of current materials in her classes, her passion for learning and personal improvement, and her effective communication skills. "There is little she wouldn't do for her students," said her team-teaching partner, Richard Seubert. "Along with high expectations, she cares for them as human beings first, which helps kids appreciate their potential and set goals that push them to higher levels. She doesn't talk down to them but promotes a dialogue which honors their ideas and celebrates their uniqueness as human beings."

In 2001, Forman received the highest honor in her profession when she was named National Teacher of the Year. The National Teacher of the Year Program is sponsored by a nonprofit group called the Council of Chief State School Officers (CCSSO) and the children's book publisher Scho-

*President George W. Bush presents Forman with the 2001 Teacher of the Year award during a ceremony in the Rose Garden at the White House, April 23, 2001.*

lastic, Inc. The process of selecting the National Teacher of the Year begins with the State Teachers of the Year. These teachers are chosen on the basis of nominations from students, teachers, principals, and school administrators. Each State Teacher of the Year must submit a written application to be considered for National Teacher of the Year. The application includes personal and career information, eight essays on topics ranging from teaching philosophy to issues facing education, and letters of endorsement. The winner is selected by a committee of representatives from 15 leading national education organizations.

The National Teacher of the Year is the oldest and most prestigious award for excellence in teaching in the United States. It has been presented annually for 50 years. Forman was the first Vermont educator to receive the honor. Her selection was announced by President George W. Bush at a special ceremony in Washington, D.C., on April 23, 2001. Forman recalled that accepting her award from the president "felt a little bit like an out-of-body experience."

The National Teacher of the Year is asked to take a year off from classroom activities in order to serve as a full-time national and international spokesperson on education. On June 1, 2001, Forman began a hectic schedule of traveling and lecturing. She looked forward to speaking out on a variety of issues that affect teachers and education. "There are a number of issues that concern me: vouchers, education funding, teacher accountability, high-stakes testing, and retaining new teachers," she stated. "Policymakers need to listen to [teachers] because we bring a perspective that no one else can."

## Speaking Out on Education Issues

During her travels as National Teacher of the Year, Forman tried to raise public awareness of a growing national shortage of qualified teachers. She pointed out that 30 percent of teachers nationwide have been teaching for 20 years or more, and that many of these teachers are expected to retire in the coming years. Yet fewer young people are training to become teachers, and 30 percent of new teachers leave the profession within three years. These factors, combined with increasing student enrollment, mean that the United States will need to recruit 2.5 million new teachers over the next 10 years.

Forman called upon the government and her fellow teachers to help address this problem by taking steps to retain good young teachers. "We know why teachers leave. They don't leave because of the money; surveys tell us they leave because of working conditions. What that usually means is an overwhelming amount of classes, or huge numbers of students in those classrooms — the lack of support and being given an impossible situation, many of our poorer schools especially," she explained. "We know how to hold teachers. We know that mentoring programs can be successful. We need to expand those. We need to demand that our schools and our communities increase those. Let's recognize that a license to teach is like a license to drive. When a new driver first gets a driver's license, it doesn't mean that he or she should set out to drive to New York City in a snowstorm, and we should not expect the equivalent from new teachers in the classroom. We are one of the few professions I know that eats its young. We fail to adequately support those joining us. We must change that."

Forman also spoke out about the need to maintain strict licensing requirements for teachers. "We must require high standards for all teachers if we want to raise the prestige of our profession and attract larger numbers of talented, dedicated people," she stated. Forman claimed that many teachers practice on waivers from basic licensing requirements, which has a strong negative effect on the quality of education they can provide. "In my state the man who gives care to my dogs cannot do so unless he is fully licensed. No waivers there. And the woman who cuts my hair cannot do so unless she is fully licensed, not on a waiver. We must educate others, you and I, to understand that teaching is just as important as engineering, medicine, veterinary medicine, and hairdressing," she said. "Can you see this now? You have an appointment with your doctor, you walk into your doctor's office, and this person comes to meet you and says, 'Hi, I'm the substitute physician. I have a high school diploma, a clean police record. I'm here to get hands-on experience.' We would not consider this in any field other than teaching, and it's time we stopped allowing it in our profession."

*"My fear is that learning is becoming standardized. Learning is idiosyncratic. Learning and teaching is messy stuff. It doesn't fit into bubbles. I don't think a simple paper-and-pencil test is going to capture what students know and can do."*

Forman also expressed her opinion about the current movement toward increased use of standardized testing of students as a way to evaluate schools and determine the level of government funding they receive. "I'm deeply concerned that the emphasis on high-stakes, multiple-choice testing is destructive," she stated. "It's gone too far. It's eating up too much of our resources. . . . It's of no value to teachers because it's not diagnostic. All it does is artificially spread out scores and rank kids. It doesn't tell me what my students can do and cannot do." Forman feels that such testing not only provides a poor assessment of student skills, but also limits teachers' creativity. "My fear is that learning is becoming standardized," she explained. "Learning is idiosyncratic. Learning and teaching is messy stuff. It doesn't fit into bubbles. I don't think a simple paper-and-pencil test is going to capture what students know and can do."

Forman thoroughly enjoyed her tenure as National Teacher of the Year. One of the things she learned from the experience was that many people have a deep appreciation for teachers. "People love teachers," she noted. "I've been on a 757 [airplane], packed with people at 39,000 feet, and when the flight attendant announced that the National Teacher of the Year is on board, the entire plane broke into applause, sustained applause. I couldn't get any work done after that, because everyone kept coming up to me and talking to me about their 'I-had-a-teacher' stories. No one on that plane knew me, but I can promise you that each person on that plane had in his or her mind a picture, a memory, of a teacher who meant a lot to him or her. I was overwhelmed by it, but I understand it. As the National Teacher of the Year, I'm a symbol for all of those wonderful teachers."

*"As a teacher, on a good day, when learning is happening, I'm a catalyst — something that allows a reaction to take place. The true power of learning is in the elements, the learners."*

Among the many other memorable moments from her term, Forman received a special tour of the National Aeronautics and Space Administration (NASA) facilities and carried the Olympic torch as it passed through Vermont on its way to Salt Lake City, Utah, for the 2002 Winter Games. "It is bittersweet," she said at the end of her year of service. "It has been a magical year." At the same time, Forman was eager to return to school. "I feel that where I make the biggest difference is working in a classroom with kids," she noted.

## Learns from Her Students

Forman attributes part of her success as a teacher to her willingness to listen to her students. She has often discarded lesson plans and started over when her students made it clear that a different approach would create better opportunities for learning. In many cases, her flexibility has produced outstanding results. "Years ago I took students to Washington, D.C.," she recalled. "One named Holly had never been out of Vermont. We went to the Lincoln Memorial and the sun was setting. We're reading the words in the stone, and Holly looks up at Lincoln and says, 'Wow! I wish we had history where we live.' Now that's a voice I needed to listen to. We went back to Vermont and swept the plate for the next quarter, suspended regular classroom activities. With a supportive administrator and parents, we set out to become historians of our county. Students started with oral

*Forman working with students.*

histories and became fascinated by old farm buildings. They took pictures, read old diaries, newspapers, county fair programs. They produced an account of agricultural history, which is now part of a permanent collection in a museum."

On another occasion, Forman was leading a discussion of the European Renaissance in her World History class. She was pushing her students to understand the concept of a renaissance — building on past learning to create something new and exciting. Then the class took an unexpected turn. "A voice from the back of the classroom, Colin, said, 'Do you think there has been a renaissance in music in the past 50 years?' For about five seconds, nobody said anything," she remembered. "Then the deluge hit

95

us. One after another, the students spilled out theories, evidence, arguments, counterarguments, displaying an astounding collective knowledge. I was amazed not only at what they knew about modern music, dwarfing my own knowledge to be sure, but at their excitement, and their deep understanding of what we mean by a renaissance. . . . They took control of the concept and constructed their learning. They owned it. It blew my lesson plan out of the water, but who needed it?"

> "The rewards I find in teaching are rooted in the joy of not only watching but also being part of my students' learning and development. I love teaching. I wouldn't trade my job for anything in the world. Each day is different. Each day I learn something new. Each day I laugh. Some days I cry. But when I wake up each morning, I know that I have one of the most rewarding and important jobs in the world, for I am a teacher."

As the end of class approached, Forman complimented her students for building on each other's ideas to develop unique insights. One of her students responded by giving credit to the teacher for allowing the discussion to flow. "That took me aback," Forman recalled. "In one light it was a bit flattering, but it was also very humbling. As a teacher, on a good day, when learning is happening, I'm a catalyst—something that allows a reaction to take place. The true power of learning is in the elements, the learners."

Despite the difficult issues facing education today, Forman finds her job tremendously rewarding. "The rewards I find in teaching are rooted in the joy of not only watching but also being part of my students' learning and development," she stated. "I love teaching. I wouldn't trade my job for anything in the world. Each day is different. Each day I learn something new. Each day I laugh. Some days I cry. But when I wake up each morning, I know that I have one of the most rewarding and important jobs in the world, for I am a teacher."

## MARRIAGE AND FAMILY

Forman lives in a century-old former schoolhouse in Salisbury, Vermont. Her husband, Dick Forman, is a semi-retired professional musician who teaches jazz piano at Middlebury College. They have three grown children. Their daughter Elissa is a psychotherapist in Massachusetts, their daughter

Laura is attending medical school at the University of Vermont, and their son Tim is a student at Hampshire College in Massachusetts.

## HOBBIES AND OTHER INTERESTS

In her spare time, Forman enjoys cross-country skiing, biking, hiking, jogging, gardening, and reading the poetry of Maya Angelou. She also likes to travel, and has shared stories with her students about her experiences in such places as West Africa, India, Korea, Greece, and Turkey. "Vermont is small, rural, and ethnically homogenous when compared with the rest of the nation," she noted. "Since I can't bring my students into the larger world on a regular basis, I bring diverse experiences and cultures to them."

## HONORS AND AWARDS

State Teacher of the Year (Vermont): 2001
National Teacher of the Year: 2001

## FURTHER READING

### Periodicals

*Burlington (Vt.) Free Press,* Mar. 29, 2001, p.A1; Apr. 23, 2001, p.A1; Apr. 24, 2001, p.A8; May 30, 2002, p.A1
*Columbus (Ga.) Ledger-Enquirer,* Feb. 25, 2002, p.C1
*NEA Today,* May 2001, p.36; Oct. 2001, p.21
*USA Today,* Apr. 23, 2001, p.D7

### Online Articles

http://www.ccsso.org/ntoy/2001/ntoy01.html
   (*National Teacher of the Year Program,* "Vermont Social Studies Teacher Named National Teacher of the Year," Apr. 23, 2001)
http://www.ccsso.org/ntoy/2001/01thoughts.html
   (*National Teacher of the Year Program,* "Thoughts on Teaching and Learning," Apr. 23, 2001)
http://www.nctr.org/content/indexpg/toy01.htm
   (*National Council on Teacher Retirement,* "National Teacher of the Year Address," Oct. 3, 2001)
http://www.uvm.edu/~uvmpr/vq/VQFALL01/teacher.html
   (*Vermont Quarterly,* "A Great Day to Be a Teacher," Fall 2001)
http://www.teachermagazine.org/tm/tm_printstory.cfm?slug=
   07inter view.h13 (*Teacher Magazine,* "Interview: Teacher for America," Apr. 2002)

Further information for this profile was gathered from interviews with Forman that aired on *The Early Show* and *CNN Live at Daybreak,* Apr. 23, 2001.

## ADDRESS

Michele Forman
National Teacher of the Year Program
Council of Chief State School Officers
One Massachusetts Avenue, NW
Suite 700
Washington, DC 20001-1431

## WORLD WIDE WEB SITES

http://www.ccsso.org/ntoy.html
http://www.vtnea.org/forman.htm
http://historymatters.gmu.edu/d/6830/

## Sarah Hughes 1985-

American Figure Skater
Winner of the Gold Medal in Figure Skating at the
2002 Winter Olympics

### BIRTH

Sarah Elizabeth Hughes was born in Great Neck, New York, on May 2, 1985. She comes from a family of athletes. Her grandfather on her father's side came from Ireland, where he played professional soccer in the 1930s. His son John (Sarah's father) was the captain of his college national championship hockey team in 1970 and even tried out for the Toronto Maple

Leafs professional team. He decided, though, that he would only make a mediocre pro player and instead became a lawyer. Sarah's mother, Amy, worked in accounting, but she became a full-time homemaker when they started a family.

John's parents had cared for foster children when he was growing up, and he and Amy wanted a large family. When he was young, John says, "there always was a baby around. Eighteen kids passed through, so we always had diapers in the house. And then I got married and we had six kids, and for 16 years there always were diapers in our house." John and Amy Hughes have six children: Rebecca, David, Matt, Sarah, Emily, and Taylor. They live in Great Neck, Long Island, about 25 miles from Manhattan. It is an upper-middle-class community known for its good schools and well-to-do residents who commute to work in New York City. Their large, eight bedroom ranch home gave plenty of room for their growing family.

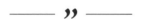

"*I was always very competitive, regardless of what it was. I tried to skate faster than [my brothers and sisters]. I always wanted to be the first to do everything.*"

### YOUTH

Sarah Hughes grew up in the midst of this large, happy family. She is often noted as being different from other figure skaters. Typically, top figure skaters live away from home so they can work with a top coach. But Sarah still lives with her family and is not the center of attention because of her skating career. All of her siblings are busy, successful young people. Her parents focus on helping all their children pursue their talents while staying normal, well-rounded people. Rebecca says, "We're not the average American family. We're all very busy. We run around. But when all of us are home, Sarah is just one of us, and that's a rare thing for an elite athlete. We're her friends." The family even has a motto — work hard and stick together.

When the children were young, John Hughes made a hockey rink in the backyard during the winter. He began teaching his boys to play hockey, as he had in college, and Sarah was invited to play, too. But she didn't like hockey — she was afraid of the puck. Still, she loved skating by herself. When she was three, her mother took her to the skating rink along with Rebecca, David, and Matt. Amy Hughes sat her four children down and began lacing up their skates, starting with the youngest first. She moved on to Matt, and then noticed that Sarah was gone. She looked out on to the crowded rink and there was little Sarah, making her way among all the whizzing skaters. "I was pregnant with Emily then, and I ran out to the rink, shouting: 'Stop that kid! She's going to get killed!' After that, I would line them up in age order and tie Sarah's skates last."

But Sarah was determined to skate — she learned to tie her own skates by the time she was four. "It wasn't so important for me to tie my skates first. It was because I was the only one who could do it right, how I liked it." When someone asked the young skater what she liked best about skating, she replied dreamily, "The ice." Skating has been important for many of the Hughes — two of her brothers have been hockey players, and two of her sisters have been figure skaters. Hughes said, "I was always very competitive, regardless of what it was. I tried to skate faster than [my brothers and sisters]. I always wanted to be the first to do everything."

## EDUCATION

Since Hughes was a young girl, skating and school have been the two major features of her life. She likes school and is a good student, which is important in order to keep up with the demands of competitive skating. Through junior high school, she was able to keep a fairly normal school schedule. She attended regular school most of the time and even played the violin in the orchestra, except when she was traveling for competitions and some tours. She would practice in the morning and arrive at school late, then train again for several hours after school.

But as her competitive schedule became more demanding, with appearances in major competitions around the world, Hughes was able to attend school less and less. The competitive skating season is during late fall and winter, so Hughes is often traveling then. And when the competitive season ends and she is not on the road, she spends much of her time training at the skating rink. With this rigorous schedule, coach Robin Wagner wanted her to stop attending school completely in favor of individual tutoring. But her parents wanted her to stay in school, for whatever amount of time possible. So whenever she's not traveling, she gets up early each morning and goes to school for biology, Advanced Placement history, or another class.

Hughes's self-discipline and sharp mind make her both a good skater and a good student. History teacher Susan Babkes says, "What I feel in Sarah is the same discipline she has for skating, she has for her studies. It's the person she is. She's gifted, she has discipline, and she has focus." Hughes's favorite subjects are math and science. She attends classes when she can, and stays in touch with her teachers by email, phone, and fax when she is out of town. Some subjects she studies independently, with the help of tutors. Sometimes they will meet at Starbucks, or at her home. They have to be very flexible to work with Hughes. "I've faxed lots of stuff to various hotel rooms around the country," said Babkes. "She'll be away for a month, but I'm able to give her a task, several essay questions, and she'll call or e-mail to talk about her impressions." One teacher, Maggie Goldberger, said, "She doesn't come to class . . . then when she comes she does better than anybody." Hughes's organizational skills help her stay on track with her studies. When she's traveling to competitions, she often takes school work with her, although she usually doesn't do any on the day of a big competition. She even had her SAT study book with her at the Nationals.

Hughes also catches up on her homework while in the car. When she's not traveling to competitions, she trains at a skating rink in New Jersey. She has a one-and-a-half hour commute each way to the rink. So after her early morning classes at school, she meets her coach Robin Wagner in the parking lot of the local mall to begin their commute to the rink. Skating talk is off-limits during this time, so they often discuss current events. Other times, Hughes does homework or reads assigned books like *Ethan Frome* (which she didn't like) or David McCullough's biography of John Adams. Wagner often makes phone calls with her headset cellular phone—to sets up appointments for fittings or photographs, to arrange trip details, or do other skating business.

## CAREER HIGHLIGHTS

### Early Training and Coaches

Hughes first experiences with skating took place when she was about three, with her brothers and sisters at the local rink and in their back yard. Her father said, "There were probably more snowball fights on that rink than serious skating." She remembers that "it wasn't a great rink. The ice was bumpy. We took our family Christmas picture on it once, so there are a lot of fond memories." Then Hughes began to take lessons. By age five, she was already showing great talent. She could do Axel jumps, double Salchows, and double toe loops, and even won local competitions. Her father said, "She would get on the ice and she wouldn't want to come off. And she would be the first one out there, and the Zamboni would be honking the horn to get her off."

Hughes had several coaches when she was young, before her parents asked Robin Wagner to be her full-time coach. Wagner had been doing choreography for Hughes since she was about nine, and had about 30

other students at the time. She had been a serious competitive skater herself in her teens, and she had experience in fashion and business. Hughes's parents were impressed with her abilities and her desire to make "a lady out of Sarah, and not just a figure skater." Her job would be more than just the technical training. Wagner would take Sarah to the rink each day and coach her on a daily basis, but she would also plan special coaching sessions with people who could help her work on new skills, such as a triple Axel jump. She would continue to choreograph routines, but would also plan costumes and hire costume designers. She would arrange publicity shoots when needed, coordinate Hughes's other workout and therapy sessions, and travel with her around the world to competitions. She was in charge of "the total package." It was up to her to design the strategy that would make Hughes an Olympic champion, from the spins and jumps to the sequins and the hairstyle. It was a huge responsibility and opportunity for Wagner.

The family's decision to choose Wagner as coach was an important and somewhat risky one. She was not a well-known coach with a proven track record. Most other ambitious skaters' families were willing to move across the country or divide up their families to be near the best, most famous coaches. But the Hughes family was committed to keeping Sarah at home and living the most normal life possible. Wagner lived nearby and could make that happen, while Sarah could still train competitively. It was an important connection that would be pivotal to the rest of Hughes's skating career.

## Competitive History

High-level competitive ice skating is a complicated business. The performances that the public sees require an incredible amount of work. The U.S. Figure Skating Association has eight levels of proficiency: pre-preliminary, preliminary, pre-juvenile, juvenile, intermediate, novice, junior, and senior. The senior level is the most visible. The best seniors compete at the World Championships and the Olympics. Competitions include two events: the short (or technical) program and the long (or freeskate) program. The short program requires a number of specific elements. The long program doesn't have required elements; instead, skaters are expected to show their technical and artistic skills. The judges base their scores for each portion on technical and artistic merit. For the overall score, the short program counts for less than the long program.

Hughes has been determined to master the skating proficiency levels since she was very young. Her family has a video of an eight-year old Sarah confidently telling the camera, "I want to be in the Olympics and get a gold medal. I can't wait for that to happen." Hughes started her climb to the gold medal podium with Novice competitions when she was about ten. She came in third in the North Atlantic Region, which allowed her to compete in the Eastern Sectional, where she came in tenth. The following year, in 1997, she won a gold medal at the regional and placed 6th at the sectional, but didn't advance to the Novice Nationals like she hoped. But instead of waiting to place higher at the Novice level, she decided, with her coach and family, to go ahead and move up to the Junior division. She was confident that she had the skills to do it.

**Moving Up to the Junior Division**

Hughes was training harder than ever to compete in the Junior division, the second-highest level in ladies' figure skating. Then the Hughes family received terrible news — Amy Hughes had breast cancer. They had to work together to help the family manage and to support Amy during her treatment. Older sister Rebecca began flying home from Harvard on the weekends to take care of Emily and Taylor. John worked long hours at his business and managing the children's lives and came to the hospital in the evenings. And Sarah became more determined than ever to do well at skating. She "took ownership of her own skating" at that point, her father said. She had read about Scott Hamilton, an Olympic gold medalist who beat cancer. She knew when she did well in skating it helped her mother feel better, and she was determined to win.

Entering her first Junior competition, Hughes stunned the crowd and her family by winning first place at the North Atlantic Regionals. Then she moved up to the Eastern Sectionals and won first place there, too. She was headed to her first Junior Nationals competition. But her mother could not be there to watch — she was in the hospital to have some of her own stem cells taken for transplant as part of her cancer treatment. John took his cell phone to the arena in Philadelphia and held it up so Amy could listen to the music as Sarah skated. A little while later, he called back. Sarah was in first place after the short program. Amy was thrilled, and the next day, the doctors were amazed to find that they had more stem cells from her blood than usual, so she could go home. She was able to make the trip to Philadelphia the next day in a friend's limousine to see Sarah skate the long program. Amy was in the audience as her daughter performed a beautiful program with a perfect triple Lutz/double toe jump combination, which won her the gold medal in the 1999 Junior National Championship. Amy remembers, "I'm sitting there saying this is the best medicine I ever had." And Sarah Hughes had a new nickname: Dr. Sarah.

*Hughes performs her short program during the Winter Olympics, February 2002.*

Hughes went on to win the silver medal at the World Junior Championships. She was invited to compete all over the world at events on the Junior Grand Prix circuit — the Hungarian trophy, the Mexico cup, and others. She was only in the eighth grade, and she and Wagner were traveling the world. They took time to see the sights — attending the opera in Vienna, eating sushi in Japan, shopping in Paris, and going to museums in Russia. Hughes was improving dramatically, and she was doing the five triple jumps that the senior women skaters performed. She and Wagner decided that it was time to move up again, this time to the final stage of skating: the senior division.

## Moving Up to the Senior Division

In 1999, at 13 years old, Hughes arrived at the Senior Nationals competition in Salt Lake City, Utah. She was in awe of being in the same competition as Michelle Kwan and Irina Slutskaya from Russia, the top female skaters in the world. Michelle Kwan had been the dominant U.S. figure skater for years and had given the most perfect performances in U.S. Nationals history in 1998. She had competed in two Olympics already, once in 1994 as the youngest competitor ever, and again in 1998, when she was favored to win. But the gold medal slipped from her grasp after Tara Lipinski skated a brilliant performance. Hughes was excited just to be at the Senior Nationals competition. "It was so cool. I think every girl who goes to Seniors for the first time probably walks in the dressing room and thinks, 'Oh my god! There's Michelle Kwan!' My problem was that I almost said, 'Oh my god! There's Michelle Kwan!'"

Hughes's short program was excellent, and she was shocked to find herself in second place, right after Kwan, her idol. But her long program didn't go as well. She fell twice, but then landed a triple-toe/triple toe combination that had only been done once before in national competition, by Tara Lipinski. After it was over, Hughes ended up with fourth place — a pewter medal. But the silver medalist was too young to go to Worlds, so Hughes took her place and found herself ranked seventh in the world.

Hughes's skating career continued to take an amazingly perfect upward spiral. She had virtually no set-backs. At the next U.S. championship, she took third. In three years at Worlds, she moved from seventh to fifth to third. At Skate America, she took fourth and then second twice. A big breakthrough came at Skate Canada in 2001. She took the gold medal, beating both Michelle Kwan and Irina Slutskaya. She was now a serious medal contender for the 2002 Olympics. The U.S. Nationals were held in January 2002, and all skaters had their eyes on the three spots open for women on the U.S. Olympic team. But then the skater Sasha Cohen made a spectacular come-back after being missing for months because of injury. Cohen took the silver and Kwan the gold, leaving Hughes with her second bronze medal at the U.S. Nationals. It may not have been what she wanted, but it was enough to get her to the Olympics.

**The 2002 Olympics**

The 2002 Winter Olympics were held in Salt Lake City, Utah. For Hughes, the month between the Nationals and the Olympics was frantic with preparation. Robin Wagner decided that this was Sarah's big chance. It was no time to be conservative, coming in as a young third-place finisher at Nationals. Hughes and Wagner continued to rework her faulty triple Lutz jump. Figure skate blades aren't flat—they have two edges like an upside-down u, and the Lutz must start from the back outside edge. Takeoff had been a continual problem for Hughes, and she and Wagner worked hard to correct it. They added another triple/triple jump combination, a risky move that would put Hughes ahead of the other skaters in terms of the difficulty of her program. They created a new ending for the long program, one with a more thrilling musical climax and choreography. "It made all the difference," Hughes later said about enhancing the difficulty and drama of the performance. "It was the most instrumental thing we did, and one of the greatest moves I've ever made. And one of the most risky moves. I knew it would be really great or really terrible."

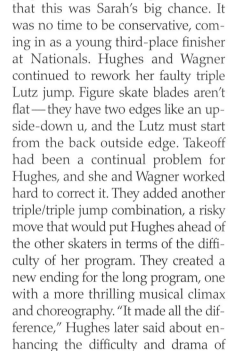

> "It made all the difference," Hughes later said about enhancing the difficulty and drama of the performance. "It was the most instrumental thing we did, and one of the greatest moves I've ever made. And one of the most risky moves. I knew it would be really great or really terrible."

In addition, Hughes and Wagner worked on her look. They ordered two additional costumes from a new designer, Jef Billings, as well as new practice costumes (the judges attend practices and take notes). Hughes had her hair cut by a new stylist in Manhattan, one known for celebrity clients. Soon the media began to pay close attention to Hughes and the other figure skaters. She was featured on the cover of *Time* magazine, while Kwan was on *Newsweek* and Slutskaya on *Sports Illustrated*.

*Hughes performs her long program during the Winter Olympics, February 2002.*

Hughes arrived in Salt Lake City to attend the opening ceremonies, where she posed with President George W. Bush for pictures. She spent two nights in the Olympic Village to get to know some of the other athletes and have some fun, then flew to Colorado Springs to spend a week training in the high altitude before her event began. During that week, controversy erupted as the judging scandal broke during the pairs event. The Canadian pairs team Jamie Sale and David Pelletier skated a clearly superior performance, yet they were awarded a silver medal. Many felt that they deserved the gold. Then the French judge admitted to being part of an agreement to "trade" votes for key performances. The world's eyes were turned on the women skaters as they began one of the final, and most watched, events of the Olympics.

## Skating the Short Program

A week of strong practices brought Hughes to the short program with a confident attitude. She went fifth, early in the evening, which is not a good position because the judges leave room in the scores for later skaters to do better. She began well, skating to *Ave Maria* with her new costume, when her first error caught her. The triple Lutz she had worked so hard on came off with the same old problem—she took off on the wrong edge of the skate. Then she came too close to the boards on the edge of the rink and had to pull her leg in to avoid colliding, which would give a major deduction. But the rest of her jumps went well, and there were no more mistakes. All in all, it was a good performance. But Sasha Cohen shone her way to third, Irina Slutskaya jumped to second, and Michelle Kwan sailed to first place with her lovely artistry. Hughes was in fourth. It meant she could still earn a medal, but that she could also come away with nothing.

*According to coach Robin Wagner, "Sarah's better as a chaser, not as the one being chased. It fires up something inside of her."*

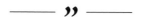

Fortunately, Hughes loves competition and a challenge. Robin Wagner said, "Sarah's better as a chaser, not as the one being chased. It fires up something inside of her." As Wagner's husband, Jerry, looked at the scores and calculated the complex scoring system, he announced that Sarah could actually still win the gold—as long as in the long program she performed absolutely brilliantly, Sasha Cohen didn't do well, and Irina Slutskaya topped Kwan's score. Sarah said, "Okay. I'll do it!"

## Skating the Long Program

The day of the long program finally came, after Hughes spent the night answering hundreds of good-luck emails and sleeping in her lucky Peggy Fleming T-shirt. She practiced, took a nap, and arrived early at the arena. Of the four top skaters, she was first again. This time, she had nothing to lose.

The music started and Hughes nailed her first two jumps—the double Axel and the triple Salchow/triple loop, her most difficult jumps. The crowd responded with roaring cheers. She was the first American to skate at the most popular event at an Olympics on home soil. In that highly patriotic year, shortly after the terrorist attacks of 9/11, the crowd was on her side. Hughes felt her confidence grow. She came to the troublesome triple Lutz and nailed it perfectly. Then she flew through another triple, and the crowd began to go wild. There was magic in the air as a superb performance began to unfold. The next triple/triple combination came, and Hughes nailed that one perfectly, too. She was the first woman to land two triple/triple combinations in competition. The audience was on its feet as she sailed through the last section of the program, to the new triumphant ending she and Wagner had worked on. She finished in a spectacular spin and then clapped and laughed in amazement as the fans cheered. She looked to her coach in astonishment—it was the most perfect performance she had ever given, at the most perfect time. Afterwards, skating enthusiasts called it a beautiful blend of athleticism and artistry, skated with a sense of freedom and joy. The performance, they said, showcased her love of skating.

Her scores were good, but with enough room to allow one of the other skaters to deliver a perfect program, too. Hughes and Wagner went to an empty locker room to celebrate and wait for the other 22 skaters to perform. A camera crew followed them in. They weren't watching the ice or even thinking about the medals at that point—they were just enjoying the moment. As the other skaters came and went, though, their attention began to turn to the ice. Sasha Cohen fell in her program—she couldn't top Hughes's score. Then the skater everyone was waiting for—Michelle Kwan. Everyone knew that Kwan was determined to win the gold medal she had missed in 1998, when she lost to Lipinski. But as she skated her program, Kwan began to make small errors. She doubled a triple jump and landed on two feet. She touched the ice as she fell out of a triple flip. The confidence drained out of her, despite the warm crowd, and she came off the ice terribly disappointed. Then Irina Slutskaya took over. She also doubled a jump and almost fell. Her performance was good, but it wasn't great. The judges tallied: Slutskaya beat Kwan, but Hughes had been brilliant. It was the one-in-a-million scenario that Jerry Wagner had described. It was the biggest upset in figure skating history. Sarah Hughes had come from fourth place to win the gold medal.

The cameraman in the locker room listened to his headset and was the first to give the news to Hughes and Wagner—Hughes had won the gold.

*The three medal winners in figure skating at the 2002 Winter Olympics: Hughes, gold (center); Slutskaya, silver (left); and Kwan, bronze (right).*

They fell on the floor laughing and crying in shock and amazement. Out in the hallway, John, Amy, and Matt Hughes were gasping in astonishment, just like everyone watching the event. Even Scott Hamilton, the sports commentator, was shouting on TV, "What an upset!" The rest of the evening, and night, went by in a rush. Hughes was interviewed, awarded her medal, and rushed to a victory party. She ended up at dinner with her jubilant family, who all wanted to see her medal immediately, at 1:30 in the morning. "I never let them stay up this late!" her mother said. Sarah said, "You know, I didn't even think it was possible. I knew mathematically it was possible, but I didn't think that could happen. I never dreamed that I'd skate so well. Although I've been training very hard for this, and I had a really good feeling about tonight. My coach and I just decided that I'd go out and have fun. I wasn't skating for a gold medal. I wasn't really skating for anything in particular. I was just skating because—just to have fun and enjoy the experience. And it was great."

**After the Olympics**

The days and weeks after the Olympics were a whirlwind. Within hours, offers were pouring in. There were so many invitations that Hughes couldn't begin to accept them all, so her father and Wagner helped her choose. She was on several of the morning news shows and Jay Leno's "Tonight Show." She hosted "Saturday Night Live," met *N Sync privately, appeared at the Grammy Awards, opened the New York Stock Exchange, and went to the White House to meet the president. She appeared on the Wheaties box, had a sandwich at her favorite deli named after her, and went home to a parade with 60,000 people cheering for her. Her first day back to school weeks later came with 60 reporters in attendance. She was so tired out that she was unable to train for the World Championships and had to miss the event. She began touring with Stars on Ice, but found that their constant circuit of cities was leaving her exhausted.

The future for Sarah Hughes looks great. Experts said that she could expect to bring in one to four million dollars in the next year and up to $10 million in the future. Another Olympic appearance in 2006 is still a possibility. And of course, with her family's emphasis on education, Hughes plans to attend college.

## HOME AND FAMILY

Hughes's self-confidence and determination undoubtedly grew out of her family's strong love, support, and work ethic. She has been very fortunate to be able to live with her family and still train as an elite skater. Other top skaters like Michelle Kwan and Tara Lipinski had to move across the country and be separated from some of their family members for years in order to work with the best coaches. Her father was opposed to Sarah moving away from home to train. "I wouldn't want her going away and just hanging around a rink when she wasn't skating. She'll do fine with her skating. It's after her skating that I'm worried about."

*"You know, I didn't even think it was possible [to win the gold medal]. I knew mathematically it was possible, but I didn't think that could happen. I never dreamed that I'd skate so well. Although I've been training very hard for this, and I had a really good feeling about tonight. My coach and I just decided that I'd go out and have fun. I wasn't skating for a gold medal. I wasn't really skating for anything in particular. I was just skating because — just to have fun and enjoy the experience. And it was great."*

*Hughes poses for photographers with her parents, after winning the gold medal.*

Hughes has received a tremendous amount of support from her whole family, but especially from her father. John Hughes uses his skills as an attorney to negotiate Sarah's contracts for tours and endorsements (Robin Wagner helps him; Sarah does not have an agent). But his first priority is being her father. He makes sure that her skating is balanced with her education and the family. His wife Amy, referring to his care for the family during her encounter with cancer, said, "He is the anchor of this ship."

Her mother's battle with cancer has had a big impact on Hughes. After the Olympics, she felt that she was in a position to speak up and to make a difference. "One of the biggest things that's happened over this year is that now I have a platform to be an advocate for causes that I'm passionate about, especially breast cancer awareness," Hughes said. "My mom, Amy, was diagnosed with breast cancer when I was 12. She was courageous and strong, and she kept going—through the first surgery, through the bone marrow transplant, through chemotherapy and radiation. She's always had a positive outlook. (Today she's been cancer-free for four years.) Seeing how well her doctors took care of her made me want to be a doctor."

## HONORS AND AWARDS

U.S. Championship, Junior: 1998, Gold Medal
Mexico Cup: 1998, Silver Medal
Hungarian Trophy: 1998, Silver Medal
World Junior Championships: 1999, Silver Medal
U.S. Championships: 1999, fourth place; 2000, Bronze Medal; 2001, Silver Medal; 2002, Bronze Medal
International Skating Union Junior Grand Prix: 1999, Silver Medal
Vienna Cup: 1999, Gold Medal
Skate America: 1999, fourth place; 2000, Silver Medal; 2001, Silver Medal
Trophee Lalique: 1999, Bronze Medal; 2001, Silver Medal
Nation's Cup: 2000, Silver Medal
Cup of Russia: 2000, Bronze Medal
Grand Prix Final: 2001, Bronze Medal; 2002, Bronze Medal

World Championships: 2001, Bronze Medal
Skate Canada: 2001, Gold Medal
Olympic Winter Games: 2002, Gold Medal

## FURTHER READING

### Books

Ashby, R.S. *Going for the Gold*, 2002 (juvenile)
Krulik, Nancy. *Sarah Hughes: Golden Girl*, 2002 (juvenile)
Sivorinovsky, Alina. *Sarah Hughes: Skating to the Stars*, 2001 (juvenile)

### Periodicals

*Chicago Tribune*, Jan. 4, 2002; January 6, 2002, p.C1; May 3, 2002, p.N1
*Newsday* Feb. 11, 2002, p B7
*Newsweek*, Dec. 31, 2001, p.87
*People*, Mar. 26, 2001, p.105; Mar. 11, 2002, p.58; Sep. 2, 2002, p.24
*Sports Illustrated*, Feb. 21, 2002, p.12; Mar. 4, 2002, p.48
*Sports Illustrated for Kids*, Sep. 2001, p.90
*Sports Illustrated Women*, Mar. 2001, p.96
*Teen People*, Nov. 2002, p.126
*Time*, Feb. 11, 2002, p.44

### Online Articles

http://www.newsday.com/sports/olympics/ny-questforgold.htmlstory
    (*Newsday*, "The Making of a Champion," multiple articles, local paper
    tribute to its local star)

## ADDRESS

Sarah Hughes
USFSA
20 First Street
Colorado Springs, CO 80906

## WORLD WIDE WEB SITES

http://www.usfsa.org
http://www.usolympicteam.com

# Enrique Iglesias 1975-
Spanish-Born American Singer
Creator of the Hit Albums *Enrique* and *Escape*

## BIRTH

Enrique Iglesias Preysler was born on May 8, 1975, in Madrid, Spain. His father, Julio Iglesias, is a well-known international singer who has sold 250 million records during his career. His mother, Isabel Preysler, is a journalist and actress who was born in the Philippines. Spanish family names are often made up of both the father's and the mother's family names, but may be shortened to just one name, usually the first of the two. That's why Enrique uses just Iglesias for his last name. He has an older sister, Chabeli, who is a talk show host on Spanish television, and an older brother, Julio Jose, who is a model, actor, and singer. He also has several younger half-siblings from his parents' later relationships.

## YOUTH

Growing up as the son of a famous singer and ladies' man was not always easy for Enrique. His father was often away from home at recording sessions or on concert tours. In fact, Julio Iglesias has readily admitted that he put his career ahead of his family. "My profession is the most important thing in my life," he stated. "If I said that my family and my children were more important, then I would be lying." Enrique's parents divorced in 1979, when he was four years old. His father moved from Spain to the United States at this time, and his mother remarried a short time later. For the next few years, Enrique and his siblings divided their time between their mother's home in Madrid and their father's home in Miami, Florida.

——— " ———

*"I remember coming to the U.S. in a huge plane, and when it landed in Miami, there were FBI agents everywhere, and we were getting picked up by helicopter, and I was like, 'Whoa, cool.'"*

——— " ———

In 1981 Enrique's grandfather was kidnapped by political terrorists. They demanded that Julio Iglesias pay a huge ransom for his father's safe release. Fortunately, Spanish authorities were able to find the kidnappers and rescue the hostage before the ransom was paid. But the incident sent shock waves through Enrique's family. They felt vulnerable and started paying greater attention to security. By 1984 Enrique's parents felt that they could no longer ensure the safety of the children in Madrid. Enrique and his siblings were sent to Miami to live with their father. "It broke my heart to send them away," his mother stated. "But we had to for security reasons."

At first, nine-year-old Enrique found the whole experience very exciting: "I remember coming to the U.S. in a huge plane, and when it landed in Miami, there were FBI agents everywhere, and we were getting picked up by helicopter, and I was like, 'Whoa, cool.'" He soon settled into his father's Miami mansion, which featured a pool and tennis courts. But he rarely saw his father, and he was raised mostly by a nanny, Elvira Olivares. "In a way, she was the closest to being a mother," Enrique noted. Before long, the young boy grew lonely. "I missed all my friends from Spain, and

*Enrique Iglesias with his parents, Julio Iglesias and Isabel Preysler, on the eve of his first communion.*

my mother, and it was pretty hard. I used to cry every single day," he recalled. "I didn't know anyone in America. It was like starting over."

In order to overcome his feelings of loneliness, Iglesias spent a lot of time at the beach and learned to love water sports, especially windsurfing. He also poured out his emotions on paper in the form of song lyrics. "I realized writing songs was the way for me to truly express myself, to let my emotions come out," he noted. "Those songs were like a diary to me. People keep their most personal thoughts in a diary, and mine were coming out as songs." Unbeknownst to his family, Iglesias had secretly dreamed of becoming a singer for many years. "I used to pray I'd grow up to be a singer," he recalled. "I'd sing along to the radio and TV, but it was stupid stuff like that that helped me to learn how to feel music. But I kept my dreams a secret and never told anybody. I strived to be independent. I matured in that way, I guess, because my dad was always working and never around, and the rest of my family was in Spain."

Iglesias loved listening to music as a teenager, though he never listened to his father's records — which contained mostly slow, romantic songs sung in Spanish. Instead, he preferred popular music by performers like Dire Straits, Billy Joel, the Police, U2, Bruce Springsteen, Marvin Gaye, and Otis Redding. "I'm one of those that can listen to so many different styles of music," he explained. "Even if I don't like it as much, there's always something I can learn." When he was 16, Iglesias began singing with a makeshift band that practiced in a friend's garage. "The songs were real cheesy. I used to cry about how bad they sounded. That was the hardest part, getting used to my voice, getting used to feeling good about what I was singing and writing. It took a long time," he recalled. "It's not like I was looking for a record deal then. I did it because I loved it. I never told anyone. For me it was a getaway to sing, one of those things I didn't want anyone to screw up."

## EDUCATION

Iglesias attended an English school in Spain, so he was able to speak English when he arrived in the United States. He acted up a bit in elementary school as he struggled to make the transition to living with his father in Miami. In fact, he was once suspended for putting a lizard on his teacher's back. But his behavior improved by the time he reached junior high.

Iglesias went to a private high school in Miami called Gulliver Preparatory School. He recalled that he was short and skinny and did not hang out with the popular crowd. Amazingly, the young man who would later be named "sexiest man in the world" by the Spanish-language edition of *People* magazine often got turned down for dates and went to the senior prom alone. "It was very hard for me to get a date when I was in high school," he noted. "I was very shy with girls and scared of being rejected. I'm still shy, I think—though it's a lot easier to get a date now."

*It's hard to believe that the young man who has been called the "sexiest man in the world" often got turned down for dates and went to the senior prom alone.*
*"It was very hard for me to get a date when I was in high school. I was very shy with girls and scared of being rejected. I'm still shy, I think—though it's a lot easier to get a date now."*

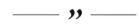

After graduating from high school in 1993, Iglesias enrolled at the University of Miami as a business major. But he had trouble concentrating on his studies because he had his heart set on becoming a singer. "I used to be in math class and it was all I used to think about," he remembered. "When I was at the university, that's all I heard in my mind." Iglesias dropped out of college during his sophomore year in order to pursue a career in music.

## CAREER HIGHLIGHTS

### Getting Started as a Singer

Throughout Iglesias's teen years, no one but his musician friends and his nanny knew that he longed to be a singer. He continued practicing in secret until he finally decided he was ready to sing in public. In 1994, shortly after he dropped out of college, Iglesias made a mysterious phone call to Fernan Martinez, his father's agent and a family friend. Without saying what he wanted, he asked Martinez to meet him. "My first reaction was: He's in trouble!" Martinez remembered. "I thought it was something with a girl, he was so mysterious and secretive. I had no clue." Iglesias took the confused agent to his friend's garage and sang several songs for him — some in English and some in Spanish. He then asked Martinez to give him an honest assessment of his skills as a singer.

——— " ———

*"It's pathetic. Even after I won the Grammy, I heard this girl say, 'Oh, you won a Grammy because your dad is Julio Iglesias.' And you know the funny thing is that last year my dad was nominated for a Grammy and he didn't win. I don't like to get into it but I'm tired of hearing, 'Do you think you sell more records because of your dad?' Well, right now in the U.S. I sell more records than my father. So it would seem a little contradictory that people are buying the records only for who my dad is."*

——— " ———

Martinez recognized that Iglesias had talent and recommended that he make a demo tape of his singing. In order to avoid telling his family about his secret passion, Iglesias borrowed money from his nanny to make the recording. He gave the tape to Martinez, who planned to play it for record company executives. But Iglesias imposed an important condition: Martinez was not allowed to tell anyone that they were listening to the son of the famous Julio Iglesias. Instead, the agent was supposed to say that the artist on the tape was an unknown singer from Columbia named Enrique Martinez. "I wanted them to buy my music, not my name," Iglesias explained. "I figured if I take the easy way, I might get there faster, but I won't last as long. People won't care if you're the son of the king of the world. If you're not good, people are not going to be listening."

After being rejected by several major record labels, Iglesias finally signed a $1 million contract with Fonovisa Records to produce three Spanish-language albums. It was only when he signed the contract that Fonovisa executives discovered his true identity. Iglesias continued to keep the secret from his family. In fact, Julio Iglesias learned about his son's record deal from a friend at a party. "He was a little shocked," Enrique remembered. "But all he told me was to do it right or not even try it at all. Besides that, so far I haven't asked him for advice, not a single time."

Iglesias released his first album, *Enrique Iglesias,* in 1995. Fonovisa supported the album with the largest promotional push ever given to a Latin singer. In fact, Iglesias did 400 interviews in a matter of months to support the launch of his debut album. *Enrique Iglesias* became a hit, selling a million copies within three months and going on to sell nearly six million copies worldwide. The album featured the hit single "Si Tu Te Vas" ("If You Go"), which reached number one on *Billboard* magazine's Latin music charts. Four songs from the album—some of which Iglesias had written in high school—eventually hit number one.

Iglesias was beginning to establish himself as a successful performer in his own right. He even won a Grammy Award in 1996 for Best Latin Pop Performance, for *Enrique Iglesias.* Yet he was often compared to his famous father, and some people even suggested that his name was the reason for his success. "It's pathetic," Enrique stated. "Even after I won the Grammy, I heard this girl say, 'Oh, you won a Grammy because your dad is Julio Iglesias.' And you know the funny thing is that last year my dad was nominated for a Grammy and he didn't win. I don't like to get into it but I'm tired of hearing, 'Do you think you sell more records because of your dad?' Well, right now in the U.S. I sell more records than my father. So it would seem a little contradictory that people are buying the records only for who my dad is."

## Reinventing Spanish Music

With the release of his first album, Iglesias became part of a new generation of recording artists. When he came on the scene, most recording artists who were singing in Spanish were older and performed mostly traditional songs. He and other singers that emerged around the same time, like Ricky Martin, adopted a modern pop sound that was faster and more sophisticated, to appeal to a younger audience.

In 1997 Iglesias followed up the success of his first album with the release of *Vivir* ("Living"), which sold five million copies worldwide. The young singer supported the album with a world concert tour that stopped in 13 countries. In 1998 Iglesias released his third album, *Cosas del Amor* ("Things of Love"). He wrote six of the songs on this album.

In 1999 Iglesias signed a $44 million recording contract with Interscope Records/Universal Music Group, making him one of the highest-paid Latino artists of all time. Under the terms of the contract, Iglesias would produce six albums—three in English and three in Spanish. He released his first English-language single, "Bailamos" ("We Dance"), a short time later. This song was featured on the soundtrack of the movie *Wild Wild West*, which starred Will Smith. The upbeat "Bailamos" became a monster hit, reaching number one on the pop charts in 16 countries. The single brought Iglesias even greater fame among American listeners and marked his emergence as a mainstream pop star.

## Reaching New Fans by Singing in English

Iglesias made a smooth transition to singing in English. "After all, I've grown up in the U.S.," he explained. "I used to write [songs] in English. My first demo was in English." He also felt that singing in English would help distinguish him from his father, who sang primarily in Spanish. Iglesias released his first English-language album, *Enrique,* in 1999. It sold seven million copies around the world and produced two number one singles. Although *Enrique* was a mainstream pop album, Iglesias claimed that

it was not too different from his earlier albums. "That's what I used to do in Spanish," he noted. "They called it Latino music, because I sang in Spanish and I'm Latino, but the albums themselves were mainstream."

*Enrique* features a cover of "Sad Eyes," a little-known Bruce Springsteen ballad. "I thought, 'What are critics going to think about me, a Latino, doing a Bruce Springsteen cover? You can't get any more American than that!'" Iglesias said. "But at the same time, I love Bruce Springsteen, and I fell in love with the song. It's such a simple song—simple and direct, but beautiful." The album also includes "Could I Have This Kiss Forever?" which Iglesias sang as a duet with Whitney Houston. Iglesias received mostly positive reviews for his English-language debut. For example, Arion Berger of *Entertainment Weekly* praised Iglesias for "an alluring voice, rich and controlled, with appealing scratched-up edges and a masterful sense of musical balance."

Iglesias experienced the ups and downs of pop stardom in the United States. On the plus side, he was invited to perform live during the Super Bowl halftime show in 2000. But he ran into controversy later that year, when outspoken radio personality Howard Stern accused him of lip-synching in his live shows. Stern even played a tape on the air that he claimed was Iglesias singing off-key. Iglesias responded by flying to New York and singing live on Stern's radio show in order to prove himself. Though he never pretended to have the best voice in the world, he wanted to make sure his fans felt that they got their money's worth. "I've always said, 'There are millions of people who can sing.' My backup singers sing better than me," he stated. "But how come they don't have solo deals? Can they really do an album and not bore you? That's really what it comes down to. It's about telling a story and having people believe it."

———— **"** ————

*"Touring is my favorite thing to do. I love the adrenaline I feel when I'm on stage and the energy I get from my fans. I love my audience. I feel so protected when I'm around them. You can't really explain what you feel. That's what pushes you. That's when you say, 'All the work, all the traveling, all the interviews, all the sleepless nights, all the hotels, all that — it's all worth it as long as you feel that."*

———— **"** ————

In 2001 Iglesias released *Escape,* his second English-language album. It sold eight million copies worldwide and produced three hit singles. One of the best-known songs from the album is "Hero," a ballad that provided comfort to many Americans in the wake of the September 11 terrorist attacks. In 2002 Iglesias released *Quizas* ("Maybe"), his first Spanish-language album in five years. "The power of music in Spanish is so strong that I couldn't stay away from it any longer," he explained. "It has been great to record an entire record in Spanish again. My fans have been by my side throughout my journey, and I hope they will enjoy taking this step with me." Iglesias wrote all but one song on the album.

### Connecting with Fans

In just a few years as a recording artist, Enrique Iglesias has sold 25 million albums worldwide. He has become tremendously popular, especially among young women. In fact, his face has graced the covers of over 250 maga-

*Iglesias performing live in Times Square in New York City, September 2002.*

zines. He claims that he enjoys all the attention he receives from fans. "Touring is my favorite thing to do. I love the adrenaline I feel when I'm on stage and the energy I get from my fans," he stated. "I love my audience. I feel so protected when I'm around them. You can't really explain what you feel. That's what pushes you. That's when you say, 'All the work, all the

125

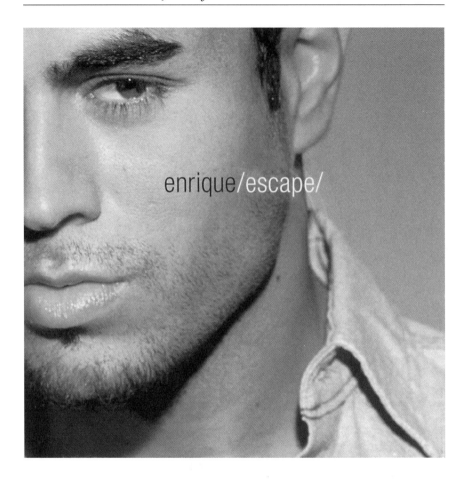

traveling, all the interviews, all the sleepless nights, all the hotels, all that — it's all worth it as long as you feel that."

Iglesias has recorded songs in Spanish, Italian, Portuguese, and English. He continues to write many of the songs he records. "Writing songs is very difficult for me," he admitted. "I am not a professional songwriter. I cannot write about a given subject, nor at any time I wish. It has to be something that has happened to me or which comes to me perhaps in a strange manner, and then I spend many hours revising what I have written, changing it until I arrive at the final result. There are many songs that die in the attempt."

Though Iglesias has earned his own spot in the music world, people continue to ask him about his famous father. He still struggles to understand why people try to make comparisons between the two singers. "If my name were Pepe Grillo, you'd never think of Julio Iglesias after hearing my voice," he noted. "Of course, there are things here and there, because I think my father is the greatest. But my thing is completely different." For his part, Julio Iglesias says that he is proud of his son's accomplishments. "I think it is amazing," he stated. "He is an amazing kid. He has a lot of class, a lot of charm, a lot of talent. Sometimes I look at him and I don't believe this guy is so young and so successful."

Enrique says he is particularly grateful to Julio for teaching him about the music business and preparing him to handle fame. "I am not impressed by money or fame. I've been lucky. I grew up around that," he stated. "I knew that if I failed I would always have something to eat. And in terms of fame and adulation I have grown up around my father. I've seen it up close, and I've learned a lot. Some people think because of that I would be even more egotistical, and it's exactly the opposite. That's my advantage. I assure you that if what had happened to me . . . had happened to a 21-year-old kid who's had nothing, it would have destroyed him psychologically."

Iglesias is thrilled to be living his boyhood dream and connecting with people as a singer. "Maybe 20 percent of the people in the world, or less, have a job they love," he noted. "I have one of the best jobs in the world. I wake up every single day and feel blessed. So I might as well keep on working as hard as possible. I gotta go all the way."

*"Writing songs is very difficult for me. I am not a professional songwriter. I cannot write about a given subject, nor at any time I wish. It has to be something that has happened to me or which comes to me perhaps in a strange manner, and then I spend many hours revising what I have written, changing it until I arrive at the final result. There are many songs that die in the attempt."*

## HOME AND FAMILY

Iglesias, who is single, lives in Miami with his two dogs. For the time being he's happy to date, but he says that he would like to get married and have a family someday. "I've been in love one and a half times, and I've had my heart broken many, many times. But I don't like to talk about that stuff," he said. "When I do settle down, though, I want to be with a girl who has a great smile, a great sense of humor, and a strong, independent streak."

## HOBBIES AND OTHER INTERESTS

In his spare time, Iglesias enjoys participating in water sports, such as windsurfing, waterskiing, and scuba diving. He donates a portion of the proceeds from his concert tours to charity, including Ronald McDonald House.

## RECORDINGS

*Enrique Iglesias,* 1995
*Vivir* ("Living"), 1997
*Cosas del Amor* ("Things of Love"), 1998
*Enrique,* 1999
*The Best Hits,* 2000
*Escape,* 2001
*Quizas* ("Maybe"), 2002

## HONORS AND AWARDS

Grammy Award (National Academy of Recording Arts and Sciences): 1996, Best Latin Pop Performance, for *Enrique Iglesias*
Latin Music Award (*Billboard* magazine): 1997, 1998, Hot Latin Tracks Artist of the Year
Sexiest Man in the World (*People en Espanol*): 1998

## FURTHER READING

### Books

*Contemporary Musicians,* Vol. 27, 2000
Furman, Elina, and Leah Furman. *Enrique Iglesias: An Unauthorized Biography,* 2000
Granados, Christine. *Enrique Iglesias,* 2001 (juvenile)
Marquez, Heron. *Latin Sensations,* 2001 (juvenile)

### Periodicals

*Billboard,* Aug. 31, 2002, p.5
*Boston Herald,* Mar. 24, 2002, p.57
*Cosmopolitan,* Jan. 2000, p.140

*Current Biography Yearbook,* 1999
*Los Angeles Times,* Nov. 29, 1995, p.F1; Nov. 23, 1997, Calendar sec., p.5;
    Dec. 2, 1999, p.F6
*Miami Herald,* Nov. 10, 1996, p.I1; Feb. 12, 1999, p.G29
*Newsday,* Mar. 15, 1999, p.B6
*People,* Apr. 22, 1996, p.144
*Rolling Stone,* Apr. 13, 2000, p.104
*Seventeen,* Jan. 2000, p.74
*USA Today,* July 14, 2000, p.E5
*Washington Post,* Jan. 28, 1999, p.C1

**Online Databases**

*Biography Resource Center,* 2002, article from *Contemporary Musicians,* 2000

**ADDRESS**

Enrique Iglesias
Interscope Records
10900 Wilshire Boulevard
Los Angeles, CA 90024

**WORLD WIDE WEB SITES**

http://www.enriqueiglesias.com
http://www.mtv.com/bands/az/iglesias_enrique/artist.jhtml

# John Lewis 1940-

American Political Leader
U. S. Representative to Congress
Leader of the U.S. Civil Rights Movement

### BIRTH

John Lewis was born on February 21, 1940, in Pike County, Alabama, in his family's rural home. He was the third of ten children born to Eddie and Willie Mae Lewis, who worked as farmers to support their family.

## YOUTH

### Growing Up Under the Shadow of Segregation

Lewis grew up during a period of U.S. history in which black Americans did not have the same rights and opportunities that white Americans enjoyed. The inferior social position of African-Americans was especially apparent in the country's southern states. This region of the country had practiced slavery until 1865, when the North defeated the South to end the American Civil War. Still, racist attitudes towards black people remained strong in many white communities. In fact, all of the southern states built political and social systems that were blatantly unfair to African-American citizens. For example, states like Alabama embraced the system of segregation, which kept white and black people separated from one another in most aspects of everyday life. The state enforced segregation in restaurants, theaters, buses, and other public places. Alabama and other states even established separate public drinking fountains for white and black people. In nearly every instance, the facilities that were designated for white people were much nicer and cleaner than those that were assigned to members of the black community. Alabama also supported separate schools for white and black children. This was perhaps the most destructive element of segregation, since these schools provided an inferior education that further limited opportunities for African-Americans.

*"Even a six-year-old could tell that this sharecropper's life was nothing but a bottomless pit. I watched my father sink deeper and deeper into debt, and it broke my heart. More than that, it made me angry. There was no way to get ahead with this kind of farming. The best you could do was do it well enough to* **keep** *doing it."*

Many African-American people resented the unequal system in which they lived. But the black communities of the American South felt powerless to change things. White men occupied nearly every important political and law enforcement office across the South, and most of them did not want African-Americans to gain greater political, economic, or social power. As a result, white officials used a variety of means to keep black families "in their place." For example, some officials forced African-Americans to pass extremely difficult written tests before they would allow them to register to vote. The poll tax—a tax that a person must pay before being permitted to vote — was another popular tool to repress the black vote, because most black people were so poor that they could not afford the expense. Finally, whites used violence and intimidation to make sure that African-Americans remained in their inferior position in society.

## A Happy Childhood

During his first years of childhood, Lewis was not aware of the segregated world that awaited him. Instead, he spent nearly all of his time playing and working on the farm that his family tended. His parents worked as sharecroppers, farming land that belonged to a wealthy white landowner. In return for the use of the landowner's property, Lewis's parents had to give the landowner a sizable portion of the profits from the sale of their crops. In addition, they had to pay the landowner for seed, fertilizer, equipment, and other materials used in farming the land. As a result, the Lewis family — like most sharecropping families — always owed the landowner money and never had much money leftover for clothing, food, or other basic needs. "Even a six-year-old could tell that this sharecropper's life was nothing but a bottomless pit," Lewis recalled. "I watched my father sink deeper and deeper into debt, and it broke my heart. More than that, it made me angry. There was no way to get ahead with this kind of farming. The best you could do was do it well enough to *keep* doing it."

*"You had to bend down to pick cotton. Eight to ten hours of stooping like that and your back would be on fire. It would ache all night, and still be aching when you got up the next morning to go out and do it all over again."*

Still, Lewis recalls his early years on the family farm with fondness. "It was a small world, a safe world, filled with family and friends," he remembered. In fact, the world of his early childhood was so small that he only saw two white people — the mailman and a traveling salesman — until he was six years old.

As he grew older, Lewis joined his older siblings out in the fields, where they spent long hours picking cotton and other crops. "You had to bend down to pick cotton," he explained. "Eight to ten hours of stooping like that and your back would be on fire. It would ache all night, and still be aching when you got up the next morning to go out and do it all over again."

Lewis also was responsible for caring for the chickens on the family farm. But unlike cotton picking, he greatly enjoyed this chore. "I named them, talked to them, assigned them to coops and guided them in every night and when one of them died, I preached his funeral and buried him," he recalled. "I also protested when one of them was killed for food. I refused to eat. I guess that was my first protest demonstration. . . . The kinship I felt with these other living creatures, the closeness, the compassion, is a feeling I carried with me out into the world from that point on."

*A picture of Lewis in the early 1960s.*

## Growing Awareness of Social Injustice

At age 11, Lewis joined one of his uncles on an extended visit to Buffalo, New York. This adventure made an enormous impression on the young boy. He was stunned to see black and white people shopping, traveling, and eating together, and was amazed to see African-American families living in clean neighborhoods lined with warm and spacious homes. "Home would never feel the same as it did before that trip," he admitted. "The signs of segregation [in the American South] that had perplexed me up till then now outright angered me."

During his teen years, Lewis sensed that black unhappiness with segregation and institutional racism was on the increase in Alabama and other southern states. In 1955, for example, civil rights activist Rosa Parks refused to give up her seat to a white person on a city bus. That action prompted civil rights leader Martin Luther King Jr. and other black citizens to organize a boycott of the bus system in Montgomery, Alabama, to protest the poor treatment they received. Elsewhere, brave black students began challenging southern colleges and universities that had long refused to open their doors to African-Americans. These courageous actions inspired Lewis to think about what he might do to advance the cause of civil rights.

In the meantime, Lewis devoted much of his time to his deep religious faith. "More than anything else — besides work, of course, which became the center of my life as soon as I was big enough to join my parents in the fields — the most important thing in my family's life, and in almost every family's life around us, was church," he recalled. By age 16, he was regularly giving sermons in black churches in surrounding communities, and he was formally ordained as a minister while he was still a teenager.

## EDUCATION

When Lewis was growing up in Pike County, Alabama, there were two separate school systems for white and black children. As was the case throughout the South, the school buildings and supplies set aside for the black children were not nearly as good as those that were available to white children. Lewis's elementary school, for instance, was a two-room wooden shack, and the schoolbooks he received were old ones that had been discarded by nearby white schools.

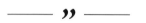

> "I loved school, loved everything about it, no matter how good or bad I was at it. My penmanship was poor—it's gotten a little better over the years, but just a little—yet the thrill of learning to write was intense."

Nonetheless, Lewis thrived in school. "I loved school, loved everything about it, no matter how good or bad I was at it," he said. "My penmanship was poor—it's gotten a little better over the years, but just a little—yet the thrill of learning to write was intense." His parents recognized his genuine thirst for knowledge, and they encouraged him to develop his reading, writing, and math skills. But the demands of farming sometimes interfered with his schoolwork. On some days, he and his brothers and sisters had to stay home from school to help harvest crops. This upset Lewis so much that he sometimes tried to sneak away to catch the school bus when no one was looking.

Lewis attended Dunn's Chapel Elementary School through sixth grade. He then completed grades seven through nine at a local junior high school. After completing ninth grade, he had few options for continuing his education since there was not a single high school in the county that was open to African-Americans. He ended up enrolling at Pike County Training School, a school that taught black youth about farming and housekeeping—careers that were seen as unthreatening to the dominant white power structure.

In 1954 the U.S. Supreme Court ruled that segregated schools were unconstitutional. "We rejoiced [at the ruling]," recalled Lewis. "It was like a day of jubilee." But this happiness did not last for long. Alabama and other Southern states defied the law and kept their schools segregated, and the federal government took little action to enforce the Supreme Court ruling and to force the Southern states integrate the schools.

In 1957 Lewis left Alabama to attend the American Baptist Theological Seminary in Nashville, Tennessee. Normally, he would not have been able to afford a college education. But the school charged no tuition. Instead, students paid for their classes by working for the school. Lewis enjoyed his classes, but he spent much of his time studying the growing civil rights movement. In 1958 he approached Martin Luther King Jr. and another civil rights leader named Ralph Abernathy with a plan to integrate Troy State in Alabama. Lewis volunteered to try to enter the school, which refused to admit black students. King and Abernathy vowed to support the young man's brave plan. But his parents recognized that the plan might put their son's life in danger, and they refused to give their consent. Their opposition killed the plan, since Lewis was still a minor.

During the late 1950s, Lewis set aside his college education in order to work in the civil rights movement. In 1961, however, he received a gift from the Southern Christian Leadership Conference (SCLC), a civil rights organization founded by Martin Luther King Jr. and others to apply the principles of nonviolent resistance throughout the South. SCLC gave college scholarships to Lewis and several other young activists. This gift enabled Lewis to attend Fisk University in Nashville, where he later earned a bachelor's degree in philosophy in 1967.

## CAREER HIGHLIGHTS

### Demonstrations and Sit-Ins

John Lewis began to emerge as one of the most influential leaders of the civil right movement while he was living in Nashville and attending American Baptist Theological Seminary. It was during that time that his interest in civil rights prompted him to attend workshops on nonviolent forms of protests. He learned how to demonstrate for equal rights in a peaceful manner. The workshops taught the activists how to respond — and how *not* to respond — when confronted by hostile opponents. The workshops also taught them how to resist in a nonviolent way, even when faced with violence. "The workshops became almost like [another college course] to students like me," he recalled. "It was the most important thing we were doing. I'd finally found the setting and the subject that spoke to everything that had been stirring in my soul for so long."

Soon Lewis joined the Student Nonviolent Coordinating Committee (SNCC), which was dedicated to ending segregation in the South. SNCC (pronounced "snick") was founded in 1960 to coordinate and organize nonviolent protests, primarily by students. With SNCC, Lewis and other young civil rights activists began participating in lunch counter "sit-ins." In these demonstrations, they would take seats at whites-only lunch counters. White reaction to these peaceful protests was swift and cruel. Lewis and other participants were taunted, insulted, and physically abused by crowds of angry white people. On many occasions, they were arrested by white police officers who charged them with disturbing the peace or trespassing. Time after time, Lewis and other brave young activists were led away to jail in handcuffs as mobs of white onlookers cheered. In fact, Lewis was arrested more than 40 times from 1960 to 1965 for participating in peaceful civil rights demonstrations. These encounters with the law horrified his family. They viewed their son's repeated arrests as a source of deep shame and embarrassment. But their disapproval failed to shake his dedication to the civil rights cause. Lewis felt that he was involved in a "holy crusade," and he saw his arrests as "a badge of honor."

> "
>
> "I will never, ever forget that moment," Lewis said about being physically assaulted as a Freedom Rider. "I was 21. I was a sharecropper's son from a farm near Troy, Alabama. Yet somehow I learned that where there is injustice, you cannot ignore the call of conscience."
>
> "

**Becoming a Freedom Rider**

In 1961 Lewis decided to work with the Congress of Racial Equality (CORE), a civil rights group that had been founded in 1942 to fight for equal rights for blacks. Lewis got involved with the group after a 1960 government decision to ban segregation in interstate travel facilities. CORE decided to test the federal government's willingness to enforce the ruling—in other words, would the U.S. government actually ensure that interstate bus and train lines were integrated. So Lewis volunteered to work with CORE and become a "freedom rider." Freedom riders were volunteers in mixed groups of blacks and whites who would board commercial buses and travel around the south to challenge segregation in buses and bus stations.

Lewis and several other freedom riders rode a bus that traveled out of Alabama into South Carolina. When the bus arrived at the small town of Rock Hill, Lewis and the others stepped down from the bus and entered

*Two blood-spattered Freedom Riders, Lewis (left) and James Zwerg (right), stand together after being attacked and beaten by pro-segregationists in Montgomery, Alabama, May 20, 1961.*

*With a taped X marking the spot where he was struck on the head, Lewis enters a police van. He and 26 other Freedom Riders were arrested in Jackson, Mississippi, May 24, 1961.*

the bus station. Despite the Supreme Court ruling, the station was still segregated — there were separate waiting rooms for black and white passengers. When Lewis tried to sit in the white waiting room, he was physically assaulted. "I will never, ever forget that moment," Lewis said. "I was 21. I was a sharecropper's son from a farm near Troy, Alabama. Yet somehow I learned that where there is injustice, you cannot ignore the call of conscience."

—————— **"** ——————

*"Courage is a reflection of the heart — it is a reflection of something deep within the man or woman or even a child who must resist and must defy an authority that is morally wrong. Courage makes us march on despite fear and doubt on the road toward justice. Courage is not heroic but as necessary as birds need wings to fly. Courage is not rooted in reason but rather courage comes from a divine purpose to make things right."*

—————— **"** ——————

Over the ensuing months, Lewis and other civil rights activists embarked on numerous freedom rides, even though they knew that they were risking their lives. Indeed, many buses carrying freedom riders were attacked by whites wielding baseball bats, firebombs, and other weapons. The rides became so dangerous that some volunteers wrote out their wills or said tearful goodbyes to loved ones before boarding buses. Even the police were no help — Lewis and other freedom riders were attacked and beaten by uniformed police officers and state troopers throughout the segregationist South. As columnist Mary McGrory noted, "Lewis [received] an unremitting diet of violence and hatred from uniformed fellow Americans. He was slammed around without mercy by sheriffs, herded into paddy wagons with electric prods, flung onto jailhouse floors, shoved, kicked, and beaten."

Yet Lewis stayed true to his philosophy of nonviolent resistance, and he never let the punishment and hatred that he experienced turn him away from his goal of establishing equal rights for African-Americans across the country. "Courage is a reflection of the heart — it is a reflection of something deep within the man or woman or even a child who must resist and must defy an authority that is morally wrong," Lewis explained. "Courage makes us march on despite fear and doubt on the road toward justice. Courage is not heroic but as necessary as birds need wings to fly. Courage is not rooted in reason but rather courage comes from a divine purpose to make things right."

*Lewis speaking to marchers at the Lincoln Memorial at the
March on Washington, August 28, 1963.*

In 1962 Lewis was named to the executive committee of SNCC, and one
year later he was elected chairman of the civil rights organization. His election surprised some people outside the group. After all, he was only 23
years old, and he did not possess an eloquent public speaking style or outgoing personality. But fellow members of SNCC admired his courage and
his faith in the principles of nonviolent resistance, and they recognized
that he possessed a fierce dedication to civil rights.

After his election, Lewis moved to Atlanta, Georgia, where he spent much
of his time engaged in fundraising activity. But he also continued to organize and participate in civil rights protests and other events. In August
1963, he joined Martin Luther King Jr. and other civil rights leaders in a
meeting with President John F. Kennedy. A few weeks later, he participated in the famous March on Washington. Hundreds of thousands of Americans from all racial and social backgrounds converged in front of the
Lincoln Memorial to show their support for civil rights and the vision of an
America undivided by racial lines. It was at this momentous event that
Martin Luther King Jr. delivered his famous "I Have a Dream" speech. But
other organizers, including Lewis, delivered impassioned speeches as well.
"By the force of our demands, our determination, and our numbers, we
shall splinter the desegregated South into a thousand pieces and put them
back together in the image of God and democracy," Lewis told the crowd

———— **"** ————

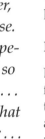

*"That was a long summer, that summer of '64. Intense. Confusing. Painful. So hopeful in the beginning, and so heartbreaking in the end. . . . For all the positive seeds that were planted that summer . . . the end result for most of the people who experienced it was pain, sorrow, frustration, and fear. No one who went into Mississippi that summer came out the same. . . . "*

———— **"** ————

to thunderous applause. "We must say 'Wake up, America. Wake up! For we cannot stop and we will not be patient!"

**Freedom Summer**

By 1964 the battle to gain equal rights for African-Americans had captured the attention of the entire nation. All across the South, civil rights organizations — like CORE, SNCC, the National Association for the Advancement of Colored People (NAACP), and the Southern Christian Leadership Conference (SCLC) — were leading demonstrations and protests calling for the end of segregation and the beginning of a new age of racial brotherhood. These activities sparked violent, hateful resistance from white political leaders and many white citizens. As clashes between the two sides became more frequent, tensions rose throughout the country. But activists knew that if their dream of securing equal rights was to come true, they had to keep pushing for change.

In the summer of 1964 Lewis and other leaders of the civil rights movement launched a new initiative called the Mississippi Summer Project. This program was a massive effort to register African-American voters in Mississippi, which had a long history of denying black people the right to vote. Such tactics as poll taxes, literacy tests, and outright intimidation were commonly used to prevent African-Americans from exercising their right to vote. The Mississippi Summer Project eventually succeeded in adding 17,000 black voters to the state's voting register. As the program got underway, the civil rights movement celebrated the passage of the Civil Rights Act of 1964. This law, signed by President Lyndon B. Johnson on July 2, 1964, prohibited segregation of public places like hotels, libraries, playgrounds, and restaurants anywhere in the United States. It also made it illegal for companies to discriminate against blacks in their hiring practices.

These developments led some people to refer to the summer of 1964 as "Freedom Summer." But as Lewis later admitted, those months also featured explosions of violence and hatred that took a heavy toll on members of the civil rights movement: "That was a long summer, that summer of '64. Intense. Confusing. Painful. So hopeful in the beginning, and so heart-breaking in the end." Indeed, over the course of the summer SNCC documented 450 violent incidents against civil rights activists and black citizens in Mississippi alone, including 30 bombings, 35 church burnings, and 80 beatings. "For all the positive seeds that were planted that summer . . . the end result for most of the people who experienced it was pain, sorrow, frustration, and fear," said Lewis. "No one who went into Mississippi that summer came out the same. So many young men and women, children really, teenagers, 18 and 19 years old, went down there so idealistic, so full of hope, and came out hardened in a way, hardened by the hurt and the hatred they saw or suffered, or both. So many people I knew personally, so many people I recruited, came out of that summer wounded, both literally and emotionally."

In 1965 civil rights leaders turned their attention to Lewis's home state of Alabama, another place where African-Americans had long been denied the right to vote. As activists spread out across the state, they organized peaceful demonstrations that aroused the fury of white communities. Sometimes these confrontations ended in episodes of ugly violence that were reported across the country. But as Lewis noted, "what tends to be forgotten among the dramatic photographs and news accounts of the moments of violence . . . were the days and days of uneventful protest that took place outside courtrooms and jails. People silently walked a picket line for hours on end, or sang freedom songs from dawn to dusk, or simply stood in line at a door they knew would not be opened, hour after hour, day after day."

*"So many young men and women, children really, teenagers, 18 and 19 years old, went down there so idealistic, so full of hope, and came out hardened in a way, hardened by the hurt and the hatred they saw or suffered, or both. So many people I knew personally, so many people I recruited, came out of that summer wounded, both literally and emotionally."*

## Bloody Sunday

On March 7, 1965, Lewis and fellow civil rights leader Hosea Williams led a group of 600 silent and peaceful marchers in Alabama. These marchers intended to walk from Selma to Montgomery to protest Alabama's re-

*At the Edmund Pettus Bridge in Selma, Alabama, on Bloody Sunday, March 7, 1965, moments before the Alabama state troopers attacked Lewis and the group. Lewis is on the right, in the light coat.*

fusal to allow blacks to register to vote. They stopped, however, when they reached a large bridge that led out of Selma — the Edmund Pettus Bridge. "There, facing us at the bottom of the other side [of the bridge], stood a sea of white-helmeted, blue-uniformed Alabama state troopers, line after line of them, dozens of battle-ready lawmen," recalled Lewis. As the marchers watched, the troopers pulled on gas masks and issued a warning to the demonstrators to turn around within two minutes or face the consequences. Lewis and the marchers responded to the threat by kneeling in prayer. One minute later, the state troopers launched a furious assault on the peaceful, praying demonstrators. The troopers ran through the kneeling marchers, swinging their batons at the heads of men and women with all their might, as reporters looked on in horror. Lewis himself suffered a fractured skull in the attack, and many other demonstrators were injured as well.

The attack in Selma quickly came to be known as "Bloody Sunday." The event was filmed by television news cameras, and it horrified the nation. The police response was so terrible and vicious that within the next few days, demonstrations in support of the marchers were held in 80 cities. Thousands of religious and lay leaders, including Martin Luther King, Jr., flew to Selma. Outraged citizens flooded the White House and Congress with letters and phone calls. Bloody Sunday convinced President Lyndon B. Johnson to send new voting-rights legislation to Congress. "At times history and fate meet at a single time in a single place to shape a turning

*Civil rights leader Hosea Williams, left, leaves the scene as state troopers break up the demonstration on Bloody Sunday. Behind him, at right, Lewis is forced on the ground by a trooper.*

*Lewis, in the light coat in the center, attempts to ward off the blow as a state trooper swings his club at Lewis's head. Lewis suffered a fractured skull in the attack.*

point in man's unending search for freedom," Johnson declared. "So it was at Lexington and Concord. So it was a century ago at Appomattox. So it was last week in Selma, Alabama. . . . Their cause must be our cause, too. Because it is not just Negroes, but really it is all of us who must overcome the crippling legacy of bigotry and injustice. And we shall overcome."

——— " ———

*"At times history and fate meet at a single time in a single place to shape a turning point in man's unending search for freedom," President Lyndon Johnson declared. "So it was at Lexington and Concord. So it was a century ago at Appomattox. So it was last week in Selma, Alabama. . . . Their cause must be our cause, too. Because it is not just Negroes, but really it is all of us who must overcome the crippling legacy of bigotry and injustice. And we shall overcome."*

——— " ———

On August 6, 1965, Johnson signed the Voting Rights Act into law. It ended literacy tests and poll taxes and ordered the appointment of federal voting registrars who would ensure the rights of black voters. Lewis attended the signing ceremony, and the president even gave him one of the pens he used in the ceremonial signing event. Years later, Lewis called the Selma campaign and the passage of the Voting Rights Act "probably the nation's finest hour in terms of civil rights."

**Leaving SNCC**

Life for African-Americans began to improve with the passage of the 1964 Civil Rights Act and the 1965 Voting Rights Act. But racism and social inequality still reigned in many areas of the United States. During this time, many black activists expressed anger with the slow pace of change. They believed that the country's major political parties and its leading lawmakers were not truly dedicated to improving the lives of African-Americans. As a result, SNCC and other black organizations turned to leaders who emphasized "black power" and independence from white society. Lewis and other civil rights activists who remained devoted to the ideals of integration and nonviolence were pushed aside.

Lewis's ouster from the leadership of SNCC took place in May 1966, when members voted to make the radical activist Stokely Carmichael the new chairman. Lewis was hurt and disappointed by the decision, but it did not shake his faith in his own beliefs. After spending several months in New

*Part of a sit-in protest in Jackson, Mississippi, June 15, 1965. Lewis, here seated (center), was among an estimated 175 people arrested..*

York, he moved to Atlanta to work as a community organizer for the Southern Regional Council. It was during this time that he met a librarian named Lillian Miles, who eventually became his wife.

In 1968 Lewis took a leave of absence from his job with the Southern Regional Council to work on Robert F. Kennedy's presidential campaign. A few weeks later, on April 4, 1968, Martin Luther King Jr. was assassinated in Memphis, Tennessee. "When he was killed I really felt I'd lost a part of myself," Lewis later wrote. Two months later, on June 4, 1968, Kennedy was shot and killed by another assassin. Lewis had greatly admired these two men, and losing both of them in the space of two months took a heavy emotional toll on him. "It hurt so incredibly much when they were taken away," he recalled. "It was like trusting yourself to fall in love again after you've given your heart once and had it broken. . . . What could we believe in now?"

In 1970 Lewis assumed leadership of the Southern Regional Council's Voter Education Project. Under his guidance, the program held voter registration drives and rallies, provided rides to courthouses and polling places for people without reliable transportation, and provided assistance to African-American politicians. In 1976, Lewis became interested in running

*Congressman Lewis speaks at home in Atlanta, January 1985.*

for Congress. Andrew Young had left his spot in the Georgia delegation of the U.S. House of Representatives to take a position in President Jimmy Carter's administration. Four years earlier, Young had become one the first African-Americans elected to Congress to represent the South in the 20th century, along with Barbara Jordan of Texas. Lewis decided to try to win Young's Congressional seat, but his first campaign for public office ended in defeat. In July 1977 Carter asked Lewis to run VISTA, a national volunteer program managed by the federal government. Lewis headed this effort for two years, then worked as a business manager in the private sector for a short time before winning election to the Atlanta City Council in November 1981.

During Lewis's first four-year term on the city council, he gained a reputation as a tireless champion of the people of his district. His high ethical standards and blunt talk sometimes produced clashes with other council members. But the citizens of Atlanta liked and respected him, and in 1985 he was elected to a second term by a large percentage of the vote.

## Dedicated Legislator

In 1986 Lewis decided to take another run at a seat in the U.S. House of Representatives. Since the district he targeted favored candidates from the Democratic Party, Lewis knew that the winner of the party's nomination would win the seat. But he faced tough competition for the seat from state senator Julian Bond, who also had been a major figure in the civil rights movement of the 1960s. Bond had the support of the Democratic Party's leadership, and his good looks and articulate manner made a good impression on television and in the newspapers. But Lewis campaigned with his usual dogged determination. "Throughout my years in the movement and throughout this new political career of mine, people had always underestimated me," he said. "With my background — the poor farm boy from the woods — and my personality — so unassuming and steady — people tended to assume I was soft, pliable, that I could be bent to meet their needs. They were always amazed, those who didn't know me, to see me dig in and stand my ground. Independence and perseverance—people had shortchanged me on those qualities all my life, often, in the end, to their dismay."

When the votes from the August 1986 primary were tallied, Bond fell just short of the 50 percent majority he needed to clinch the nomination. A runoff election was scheduled for September 2 between Bond and Lewis, who had finished second in the primary voting. Most political observers thought that Bond would claim an easy victory. But Lewis performed strongly in three televised debates and he pulled off what the *New York Times* described as "a stunning upset." Two months later, Lewis defeated Republican candidate Portia Scott to claim his place in the U.S. Congress.

In January 1987 Lewis was sworn in as a member of the 100th Congress in the U.S. House of Representatives. He has remained a member of Congress ever since, winning re-election eight consecutive times. "I have continued to tend to the hands-on needs of my constituents [during that time]," Lewis wrote. "But beyond that, my overarching duty, as I declared during that 1986 campaign and during every campaign since then, has been to uphold and apply to our entire society the principles which formed the foundation of the movement to which I have devoted my entire life, a movement I firmly believe is still continuing today. I came to Congress with a legacy to uphold, with a commitment to carry on the spirit, the goals, and the principles of nonviolence, social action, and a truly interracial democracy. . . . [Government's] first concern should be the basic needs of its citizens—not just black Americans but *all* Americans—for food, shelter, health care, education, jobs, livable incomes, and the opportunity to realize their full potential as individual people."

*"[As a representative to Congress], my overarching duty, as I declared during that 1986 campaign and during every campaign since then, has been to uphold and apply to our entire society the principles which formed the foundation of the movement to which I have devoted my entire life, a movement I firmly believe is still continuing today. I came to Congress with a legacy to uphold, with a commitment to carry on the spirit, the goals, and the principles of nonviolence, social action, and a truly interracial democracy."*

147

Throughout his years in Washington, Lewis has been a quiet but steady advocate for Americans who are poor and politically powerless. He admits that other politicians are better at grabbing the spotlight and making speeches. But he feels that his own low-key style has been effective as well. "People who are like fireworks, popping off right and left with lots of sound and sizzle, can capture a crowd, capture a lot of attention for a time," he acknowledged. "But I always have to ask, where will they be at the end? Some battles are long and hard, and you have to have staying power. Firecrackers go off in a flash, then leave nothing but ashes. I prefer a pilot light—the flame is nothing flashy, but once it is lit, it doesn't go out."

—— " ——

*"People who are like fireworks, popping off right and left with lots of sound and sizzle, can capture a crowd, capture a lot of attention for a time. But I always have to ask, where will they be at the end? Some battles are long and hard, and you have to have staying power. Firecrackers go off in a flash, then leave nothing but ashes. I prefer a pilot light—the flame is nothing flashy, but once it is lit, it doesn't go out."*

—— " ——

At times, Lewis's refusal to compromise on his life-long pursuit of peace and racial unity has led him to take unpopular positions on certain issues. For example, he was one of the few in Congress who voted against the 1991 Persian Gulf War. He also refused to participate in the October 1995 Million Man March on Washington. In this event, which was organized by Nation of Islam leader Louis Farrakhan, hundreds of thousands of African-American men from around the country gathered in Washington to renew their dedication to their families and communities. But to Lewis and many others, Farrakhan's history of racist statements cast a shadow over the event. "I supported the ideas and goals of that march," said Lewis. "I did not march because I could not abide or overlook the presence and central role of Louis Farrakhan, and so I refused to participate. I believe in freedom of speech, but I also believe that we have an obligation to condemn speech that is racist, bigoted, anti-Semitic or hateful. Regardless of the race of the speaker, I won't be a party to it. . . . I am committed to bringing the people of this nation together, not pushing them apart."

*Lewis and President Bill Clinton at an event commemorating the 1963 March on Washington, August 26, 1998.*

## Walking with the Wind

In 1998 Lewis published an autobiography called *Walking with the Wind: A Memoir of the Movement*. The book was warmly received by readers and critics across the country. The *Washington Post* described it as a "definitive account of the civil rights movement" and claimed that "it is impossible to read this inspirational and hideous story of courage and cruelty without being moved." Writing in the *Los Angeles Times*, Jack Nelson offered similar praise for the book and its author: "A shy, humble man of deep convictions, Lewis lacked the charisma of such civil rights figures as [Martin Luther King Jr.], Jesse Jackson, Julian Bond, and Stokely Carmichael. Yet his compelling autobiography, *Walking with the Wind*, helps us understand how this son of poor Alabama sharecroppers not only survived the turbulent 1960s but rose to become a heroic figure and an influential member of Congress." Nelson went on to say that *Walking with the Wind* is "destined to become [a classic] in civil rights literature." In 1999 *Walking with the Wind* won the Robert F. Kennedy Book Award. In announcing the award, the chair of the selection committee described Lewis's book as "an honest and trenchant memoir that powerfully conveys the anguish and hope of tragic days. It is both a superb contribution to the history of our times and a moving evocation of a gallant spirit."

———— " ————

*"There is an old African proverb: 'When you pray, move your feet.' As a nation, if we care for the Beloved Community, we must move our feet, our hands, our hearts, our resources to build and not to tear down, to reconcile and not to divide, to love and not to hate, to heal and not to kill. In the final analysis, we are one people, one family, one house — the American house, the American family."*

———— " ————

Honors for Lewis's long and distinguished record of civil rights activism and public service continued in 2002. In that year, he received both the Martin Luther King Memorial Award from the National Education Association and the prestigious Spingarn Medal from the NAACP. The Chairman of the NAACP, Julian Bond — Lewis's old civil rights ally and political opponent — declared that Lewis was a worthy recipient for the honor. Bond described him as "a true American hero" whose "bravery and solid commitment to justice and dignity are legendary."

Lewis appreciates the recognition he has received in recent years. He is also proud of the progress that the United States has made in improving race relations and addressing social problems. "No one, but no one, who was born in America 40 or 50 or 60 years ago and who grew up and came through what I came through, who witnessed the changes I witnessed, can possibly say that America is not a far better place than it was," he said. But Lewis recognizes that there is still a lot more work to be done. "There is an old African proverb: 'When you pray, move your feet,'" he said. "As a nation, if we care for the Beloved Community, we must move our feet, our hands, our hearts, our resources to build and not to tear down, to reconcile and not to divide, to love and not to hate, to heal and not to kill. In the final analysis, we are one people, one family, one house — the American house, the American family."

## MARRIAGE AND FAMILY

John Lewis married Lillian Miles on December 21, 1968, in a ceremony officiated by the Reverend Martin Luther King Sr. She currently serves as an administrator for the Office of Research and Sponsored Programs at Clark-Atlanta University. They have one son, John Miles Lewis, whom they adopted in 1976.

## HOBBIES AND OTHER INTERESTS

Lewis enjoys collecting antiques and rare books about African-Americans.

## WRITINGS

*Walking with the Wind: A Memoir of the Movement,* 1998 (with Michael D'Orso)

## HONORS AND AWARDS

Best Nonfiction Book of the Year (*Booklist*): 1998, for *Walking with the Wind*
Robert F. Kennedy Book Award: 1999, for *Walking with the Wind*
Four Freedoms Award (Franklin and Eleanor Roosevelt Institute): 1999
John F. Kennedy Profile in Courage Award for Lifetime Achievement (John F. Kennedy Library): 2001
Martin Luther King Memorial Award (National Educational Association): 2002
Spingarn Medal (National Association for the Advancement of Colored People — NAACP): 2002

## FURTHER READING

### Books

*Contemporary Black Biography,* Vol. 2, 1992
Egerton, John. *A Mind to Stay Here: Profiles from the South,* 1970
*Encyclopedia of World Biography,* 1998
Halberstam, David. *The Children,* 1998
Hampton, Henry, and Steve Fayer. *Voices of Freedom: An Oral History of the Civil Rights Movement from the 1950s through the 1980s,* 1991
Hill, Christine M. *John Lewis: From Freedom Rider to Congressman,* 2002 (juvenile)
Kennedy, Caroline, ed. *Profiles in Courage for Our Time,* 2002
Lewis, John, and Michael D'Orso. *Walking with the Wind: A Memoir of the Movement,* 1998
McGuire, William, and Leslie Wheeler. *American Social Leaders,* 1993
*Who's Who in America,* 2002

### Periodicals

*Atlanta Journal-Constitution,* Dec. 4, 1994, p.E1; Mar. 8, 1999, p.A3; Apr. 24, 1999, p.E2; June 29, 2000, p.J3; Apr. 8, 2002, p.C1
*Christian Century,* July 15, 1998, p.689

*Current Biography Yearbook,* 1980
*Dissent,* Winter 1997, p.9
*Ebony,* July 1967, p.146; Oct. 1971, p.104; Nov. 1976, p.133; Oct. 1999, p.182
*Jet,* Dec. 28, 1998, p.14; June 11, 2001, p.4; July 15, 2002, p.4
*Los Angeles Times,* June 14, 1998, p.5
*National Geographic,* Feb. 2000, p.98
*New Leader,* June 29, 1998, p.20
*New Republic,* July 1, 1996, p.19; Oct. 5, 1998, p.12
*New York Times,* Sep. 4, 1986, p.A1; July 6, 1991, p.A8; Mar. 8, 1999, p.A12
*New York Times Magazine,* June 25, 1967, p.5
*Newsweek,* June 1, 1998, p.69
*Parade,* Feb. 4, 1996, p.8
*People,* Aug. 24, 1998, p.125
*Time,* Aug. 4, 1986, p.26
*Washington Monthly,* May 1998, p.38
*Washington Post,* Sep. 7, 1986, p.C7; June 9, 1998, p.D1; Mar. 6, 2000, p.C1

## Online Articles

http://www.cs.umb.edu/jfklibrary/newsletter_summer2001_07.html
   (*John F. Kennedy Library and Foundation Newsletter,* "Remarks by John
   Lewis," Summer 2001)
http://www.time.com/time/community/transcripts/1999/022399lewis.html
   (*Time.com,* Transcript of interview with John Lewis, Feb. 23, 1999)

## Online Databases

*Biography Resource Center Online,* 2002, articles from *Contemporary Black
   Biography,* 1992, and *Encyclopedia of World Biography,* 1998

## ADDRESS

John Lewis
343 Cannon
Washington, DC 20515

## WORLD WIDE WEB SITES

http://www.house.gov/johnlewis
http://memory.loc.gov/ammem/today/mar07.html
http://www.pbs.org/newshour/forum/july98/lewis.html

# Andy Roddick 1982-

American Professional Tennis Player
Winner of Five Career Association of Tennis
Professionals (ATP) Tournaments

## BIRTH

Andy Roddick — known to his friends as "A-Rod" — was born
on August 30, 1982, in Omaha, Nebraska. His father, Jerry, was
a private investor and businessman. His mother, Blanche, was
a schoolteacher and homemaker. He has two older brothers,
Lawrence and John.

## YOUTH

Roddick's family moved to Austin, Texas, when he was five years old. But Andy still considers Omaha his hometown. "It's small-town USA, I guess," he stated. "I was brought up with good family values. You won't find people there with a lot of attitude, I'm pretty laid back mentally. I haven't been back to Nebraska for a few years now, what with all the traveling, but I suppose there's a lot of the state still in me."

### Older Brothers Fire Competitive Instincts

Roddick grew up in a competitive family that enjoyed all kinds of sports. Both of his older brothers were good athletes, and Andy followed them around and tried to imitate them from an early age. His brother Lawrence was a competitive diver who eventually made the U.S. Senior National Team. Young Andy often accompanied him to the pool and jumped off of the 30-foot-high diving platform. "I would see him do it and try to copy him," he remembered. "Of course, it would usually end up with me doing a belly flop."

His brother John was an outstanding junior tennis player. Inspired by John's success, Andy began taking tennis lessons at the age of six, and he played in his first tournament a year later. He also spent hours in the garage playing imaginary matches against the great professional tennis players of the era. "Oh yeah, I destroyed all the big names — [Pete] Sampras, Andre Agassi, Boris Becker, you name it," he recalled. "Of course I did it when I was eight, practicing in my garage."

In 1993, the Roddick family moved from Austin to Boca Raton, Florida, so that John could attend a tennis academy and play year-round. Andy attended many of his brother's matches and dreamed of equaling his accomplishments. "I remember being in the newspaper once when they took a picture of him and I was in the background," he noted. "I was all stoked because my hat was in the picture. I was like, 'Yeah man, I'm famous!'" John Roddick went on to become a three-time all-American at the University of Georgia. Although John's hopes for a professional career were ended by a back injury, he became a successful college tennis coach.

### A Rising Star in Junior Tennis

When the Roddick family moved to Florida, 11-year-old Andy began concentrating on tennis as well. For a while he trained under Rick Macci, a well-known tennis coach who contributed to the early development of top women's players Venus and Serena Williams. Although Roddick became a star in junior tennis, his parents made sure that he kept his feet on the ground. His mother, in particular, would not tolerate bad manners and once pulled Andy off the court in the middle of a match. "I would say it was the most embarrassing day I've ever had," he remembered. "I was 12, I guess, and I was playing this kid I didn't like. I thought he'd cheated once before. I just did not like this kid at all. I lost the first set and this kid was really annoying. So he runs up to the net, hits a little ball, and I hit it as hard as I can right at him. But he ducks and it goes out. And instead of calling it out, he gives me the finger. This drove me nuts. I lost it. 'I hate you! You're so mean!' I was shouting. I couldn't express my anger. So Mom came up and said: 'All right, you're off the court.'"

As Roddick made his way up through the ranks of junior tennis, his main goal was to earn a college scholarship, like his brother had done. But in 1998 two factors combined to make Roddick raise his goals. First, he started an impressive growth spurt that added almost a foot to his height, which improved his chances of becoming a professional tennis player. Second, he began working with a new coach, Tarik Benhabiles. "It was during a rain delay at the American Junior Nationals," Roddick recalled of the chance first encounter with Benhabiles. "Mom and I were sitting under the same canopy as him. We just starting talking and it turned out he lived three streets away from me." Benhabiles had reached the top 20 himself on the professional tennis tour and had also coached French pros Cedric Pioline and Nicolas Escude into the world rankings.

> "I would say it was the most embarrassing day I've ever had. I was 12, I guess, and I was playing this kid I didn't like. I thought he'd cheated once before. I just did not like this kid at all. I lost the first set and this kid was really annoying. So he runs up to the net, hits a little ball, and I hit it as hard as I can right at him. But he ducks and it goes out. And instead of calling it out, he gives me the finger. This drove me nuts. I lost it. 'I hate you! You're so mean!' I was shouting. I couldn't express my anger. So Mom came up and said: 'All right, you're off the court.'"

With the help of Benhabiles, Roddick made rapid improvements in both his mental and physical game. "It's so important to have the right people, to be around positive people," said his mother. "The kid has to look in his coach's eyes and has to see that he believes in him." Benhabiles felt that his new student had the potential to be a solid professional tennis player. "He has no holes in his game. He is a powerful player but also has finesse in his game. He moves unbelievably well for his size," the coach said. "Andy's work ethic and his intensity level are tremendous for a kid his age. I tell him not to worry about the future, because if his dedication stays the same, there's no limit."

*"I was the class clown at high school. Smart comments and stuff. There was this one teacher that would make me write 500-word essays as punishment whenever I spoke out of turn or did something bad. So one Sunday I decided I'd write five or six of 'em and when she said, 'Write, 500-word essay!' I just pulled one right out of my desk. She made me write 1,000 for that one."*

## EDUCATION

Roddick attended a private high school called Boca Prep. He maintained a 3.5 grade point average, even though he freely admits he was "not the most studious guy in the world." Roddick was a popular student who often entertained his classmates and annoyed his teachers. "I was the class clown at high school," he recalled. "Smart comments and stuff. There was this one teacher that would make me write 500-word essays as punishment whenever I spoke out of turn or did something bad. So one Sunday I decided I'd write five or six of 'em and when she said, 'Write, 500-word essay!' I just pulled one right out of my desk. She made me write 1,000 for that one."

Against the advice of his tennis coach, Roddick played on his school's varsity basketball team. In fact, he once snuck out of his parents' house to play in a big game. "I looked at the newspaper the next day and there was Andy's name," his mother remembered. "Zero points. Five rebounds. Hmm. And he told me he was just going out with his friends for a while." Roddick graduated from Boca Prep in May 2000. Although tennis commitments forced him to miss his graduation ceremony, he did attend the senior prom, where he was named Prom King. After graduation, Roddick put his college plans on hold to play professional tennis.

*Roddick returning a serve at the Monte Carlo Tennis Open, April 2002.*

## CAREER HIGHLIGHTS

### Turning Pro

By the time Roddick turned professional during the 2000 season, he had already gained a reputation as one of the biggest servers in the game. His serves sometimes reached speeds of 140 miles per hour, and some observers claimed that he might someday beat Greg Rusedski's record serve of 149 miles per hour. In addition to his overpowering first serve, Roddick had a strong second serve, a good baseline game, and a high-energy, enthusiastic court presence.

In 2000, Roddick appeared in some professional tournaments while also continuing to play junior tennis. At one professional tournament in Washington, D.C., he defeated players ranked 24th, 61st, and 89th in the world before losing to Agassi in the quarterfinals. By the end of the year, Roddick's world ranking had rocketed from 800 to 160. Meanwhile, he won the junior division of the Australian Open and the U.S. Open. These two events, along with the French Open and Wimbledon, make up the Grand Slam of tennis, the most presigious events on the pro tour. He also finished the season as the world's top-ranked junior player, becoming the first American man to achieve this feat in eight years.

In 2001 — his first full season on the professional tennis tour — Roddick earned a string of impressive victories that convinced some observers that he represented the future of American men's tennis. The first indication of his talent came in March, when he defeated Pete Sampras at the Ericsson Open in Miami, Florida. Sampras had won a record 13 Grand Slam titles over the course of his 13-year career, making him one of the best tennis players in history. Roddick admitted that it felt strange to face one of his childhood idols across the net. "I was trying to keep it just another match," he recalled. "Then, during the warm-up, I kind of sneaked a look over the net and thought, '*Oooohhh-kaaayyy*, I'm playing Pete Sampras, in front of 15,000 people, and it's on national television.'"

Roddick quickly overcame his nerves and began blasting away with his powerful serve. Over the course of the match, he hit seven aces, winning serves that go untouched by the opposing player. Some of his serves were so fast that Sampras was unable to get out of the way. "He just throws it up and swings as hard as he can," Sampras noted. "A couple of them went into my body, just kind of caught me off guard. He really can crack it pretty good." To the amazement of the crowd, Roddick dominated the match and went on to become the first player outside the top 100 to beat Sampras in seven years. Afterward, Sampras had nothing but praise for the rookie: "The way he played today, the future of American tennis is looking very good. The way he competes and the way he plays, he really is the future." But Roddick tried to deflect some of the praise. "I'm not a hero. I'm a tennis player," he stated. "I'm not the president or anything special. Pete Sampras and Andre Agassi are still my heroes."

### Claiming His First Professional Tournament Victory

In April 2001, Roddick won his first professional tournament at the Verizon Tennis Challenge in Atlanta, Georgia. He claimed the title in only his tenth event as a pro — faster than such American greats as Agassi, Sampras, Michael Chang, or Jim Courier. "Last year, I was going in to compete. I was basically going to the court to take my beating and then leave," Roddick said afterward. "This year, I thought if I played well and stuck around, I could get some opportunities, and I did."

Roddick proved that the victory had been no fluke a week later, when he captured his second career title at the U.S. Men's Clay Court Championships in Houston, Texas. Roddick learned about the power of crowd support at this tournament, when his semifinal match was interrupted by a several-hour rain delay. "Finally, at 11 p.m., we got back out to finish and there were still about 250 fans, all psyched to see the end of the match," he remembered. "I was feeling sluggish, not into playing, until I saw those fans. Then all of a sudden I really wanted to win. They got me pumped. I won . . . and as I signed autographs, the fans were thanking me. I thought it should be the other way around. Something clicked in my head. Maybe I could thank them—in a different way. So I got the umpire's mike and announced that anyone who didn't have a ticket for the final the next day should go and pick one up at the box office on the way out, that it was on me."

At the French Open, his first Grand Slam event of the year (he did not play in the earlier Australian Open), Roddick played an epic second-round match against fellow American Michael Chang. Chang had won the French Open title 12 years earlier by overcoming terrible cramps to defeat Ivan Lendl. "One of the matches that got me interested in tennis was the one here between Michael and Ivan Lendl —you know, where Michael started cramping so badly, he served underhand," Roddick recalled. "But he hung in and won and went on to become the youngest player to win the French Open. That was 1989. I was six."

Strangely, history seemed to repeat itself during the match. Roddick began experiencing severe cramps during the fifth set, but he showed great determination and won the four-hour

> Roddick admitted that it felt strange to face one of his childhood idols across the net. "I was trying to keep it just another match. Then, during the warm-up, I kind of sneaked a look over the net and thought, 'Oooohhh-kaaayyy, I'm playing Pete Sampras, in front of 15,000 people, and it's on national television.'"

contest by a score of 5-7, 6-3, 6-4, 6-7 (5-7), 7-5. (In men's tennis, a player wins a match by defeating his opponent in 3 of 5 sets—except in the early rounds of some tournaments, when he must win 2 of 3 sets. The first player to win 6 games usually wins the set, but if the margin of victory is less than 2 games, the set is decided by a tie-breaker. Shorthand notation is often used to show the score of a tennis match. For example, 6-2, 4-6, 7-6 means that the player in question won the first set by a score of 6 games to 2, lost the next set 4 games to 6, and came back to win the match in a third-set tie-breaker.) Roddick hit a tournament record 37 aces during the match against Chang. "Relief, joy, you can't even explain moments like that," he said afterward. "I almost wanted to cry, but I wanted to scream

*Roddick at Wimbledon, June 2002.*

and yell at the same time. That's what I play tennis for." Unfortunately, Roddick pulled a hamstring muscle during his third-round match against Lleyton Hewitt and was forced to retire from the tournament.

At the 2001 Grand Slam event at Wimbledon, Roddick lost in the third round to eventual winner Goran Ivanisevic. In August Roddick claimed his third career title at a tournament in Washington, D.C. Later that month he made it to the quarterfinals of the U.S. Open before suffering a heartbreaking five-set loss to eventual winner Lleyton Hewitt, 6-7 (7-5), 6-3, 6-4, 3-6, 6-4. Roddick was trailing in the fifth set when he hit a backhand that TV replays showed landed in his opponent's court. The line judge called the ball correctly, but umpire Jorge Dias overruled the call from his chair on the other side of the court. Roddick was outraged at what he felt was an irresponsible decision by the umpire. He went crazy on the court, yelling at the umpire and calling him a "moron." "That's the worst I've ever lost it on a tennis court, but I had a good reason to. He can't overrule that ball in that situation," Roddick explained. "No umpire in his right mind would make that call. That's not a ball he can say—and this is the rule of umpires—'I saw it clearly, 100 percent, no doubt in my mind out.' If he can say that, he's a liar." The bad call threw off Roddick's concentration, and he lost the match a short time later.

Although the 2001 season held its share of disappointments for Roddick, he still performed remarkably well for such a young player. He claimed the first three tournament titles of his career, and he saw his world ranking rise from 160 to 16. He thus became the first American teenager to be ranked in the top 20 since Michael Chang a decade earlier. He was also selected to represent the United States as part of the Davis Cup team, which played a series of tournaments against other countries. Roddick won the only match he played and became friends with several other American players, including Jan-Michael Gambill and Andre Agassi.

## Continuing to Learn and Improve

Roddick started off the 2002 season with a bang, claiming his fourth career singles title in February at the Kroger St. Jude tournament in Memphis, Tennessee. He also played well on the Davis Cup team, winning his first seven matches of the year and clinching a victory for the American team over Spain. Roddick helped boost the Americans into the semifinals, where they lost to a strong French team. In April 2002 Roddick captured his fifth tournament victory in Houston, Texas, defeating Pete Sampras in the final.

Despite his success in lesser tournaments, some critics claimed that Roddick would not be considered among the top names in tennis until he won a Grand Slam event. But Roddick's string of bad luck continued in the 2002 Grand Slam tournaments. He was forced to retire in the second round of the Australian Open with an ankle sprain, then he lost in the first round at the French Open and in the third round at Wimbledon. "In Grand Slam, I just haven't put it together," he admitted. "But there's still some tennis to be played this year. I'm going to get back to the drawing board and see what I can do with the rest of it."

By August 2002, Roddick had broken into the top 10 in the world rankings. He played well at the U.S. Open and reached the quarterfinals, where he faced Pete Sampras. Fans and the media eagerly anticipated this match, which was billed as a battle between the current and future generations of American men's tennis. By that time Sampras had gone two years without winning a Grand Slam title, and some people wondered whether the aging champion's skills were fading. "I'm excited about playing Pete," Roddick said. "We're from the same country, from kind of generations that are overlapping. I grew up idolizing him. I have a great deal of respect for Pete and what he's done. It will be a very special moment for me out there. But, you know, having said that, I want to go out there and play some ball."

Unfortunately for Roddick, the match was a bit of a letdown. Sampras proved his critics wrong and easily defeated the younger player in straight sets, 6-3, 6-2, 6-4. "It's a learning experience," Roddick said afterward. "I'll try my best to soak it up. I'll have my moment here someday. I'll have to keep working hard and take something away from these losses, as well as the wins." Sampras went on to win the U.S. Open championship — the 14th Grand Slam of his remarkable career.

> **"**
>
> *"I'm excited about playing Pete [Sampras]. We're from the same country, from kind of generations that are overlapping. I grew up idolizing him. I have a great deal of respect for Pete and what he's done. It will be a very special moment for me out there. But, you know, having said that, I want to go out there and play some ball."*
>
> **"**

### High Hopes for the Future

As the 2002 season came to a close, Roddick had posted a career singles record of 98-40, with five titles and $1.8 million in prize money. He considers himself fortunate to be able to make a living as a professional tennis player. "It is definitely something I dreamt about growing up," he stated. "I never thought it would come true, but now that it has I will never take a day of it for granted." Roddick has won over many tennis fans with his laid back style and his fun-loving, enthusiastic approach to the game. "I'm not good when I keep everything pent up inside," he explained. "I'm an emotional player. I'm sure I'll never be one of those players who never say anything. I like to leave it out there."

Despite his early success, Roddick remains committed to working hard and improving his game. "The fact that I am doing ok on tour now but feel that I have a lot of room for improvement keeps me optimistic about the future," he noted. "I don't know what the future holds. Your guess is as good as mine. But if I don't make it as big as Pete and Andre, which I probably won't, considering they're two of the greatest ever, I just said it's not going to be because of lack of hard work or effort on my part."

*A smashing serve at the Mercedes-Benz Cup, July 2002.*

Many observers have commented that Roddick has the potential to fill the gap that will be left in men's tennis when the current generation of stars retire. "Andy will certainly help the men's game, because we all know the men's game can use a big kick in the butt," said Patrick McEnroe, captain of the U.S. Davis Cup team. "I think we're all wondering what's going to happen when Agassi and Sampras are gone — and Andy could be it. He has so much raw energy and enthusiasm. He enjoys the pressure and the challenge. He has the pizzazz." Although Roddick would love to achieve

163

the success of his idols, he is determined to play his own game. "I said all along that I'm not going to replace Sampras and Agassi," he stated. "I'm going to try to do my own thing and hope that works out well."

## HOME AND FAMILY

Roddick recently purchased a home in a gated community near Boca Raton. His top priority was peace and quiet, so he appreciates the fact that most of his neighbors are senior citizens. Roddick remains close to his parents and calls home often when he is traveling. "Whenever I need advice I first go to my parents," he stated. "For sure."

> "Andy will certainly help the men's game, because we all know the men's game can use a big kick in the butt," said Patrick McEnroe, captain of the U.S. Davis Cup team. "I think we're all wondering what's going to happen when Agassi and Sampras are gone — and Andy could be it. He has so much raw energy and enthusiasm. He enjoys the pressure and the challenge. He has the pizzazz."

Roddick, who is single, claims that his lifestyle leaves little time for dating. "I'm starting to see how playing tennis around the globe doesn't exactly help the boyfriend-girlfriend thing," he admitted. "I'm not about to get married, but it would be great to have someone who I could just [hang out] with after matches."

## HOBBIES AND OTHER INTERESTS

In his spare time, Roddick enjoys playing golf and basketball, riding mountain bikes and jet skis, listening to music, and shopping for furniture and decorations for his new house. He also likes watching sports on TV and is a big fan of the University of Nebraska Cornhuskers football team.

Roddick's good looks, outgoing personality, and success on the court have provided him with many opportunities outside of tennis. For example, he made a guest appearance on the TV series "Sabrina, the Teenage Witch," in which he taught star Melissa Joan Hart to play tennis. Roddick was included on *Us* magazine's list of the world's sexiest athletes, and he placed in the top 10 of a poll of the most marketable athletes in sports. His current sponsors include Reebok, Babalot rackets, Sports Authority, and Pristine trading cards.

## FURTHER READING

### Periodicals

*Daily Telegraph* (London), June 25, 2001, p.65
*Fort Lauderdale Sun-Sentinel,* Dec. 13, 1999, p.D12
*Houston Chronicle,* Apr. 21, 2002, p.1; Apr. 29, 2002, p.1
*Los Angeles Times,* Apr. 2, 2001, p.D5; June 2, 2001, p.D5; June 28, 2001,
    p.D7; July 15, 2001, p.D1; July 22, 2001, p.D3; Sep. 7, 2001, p.D1; Sep. 6,
    2002, p.D1
*Miami Herald,* Dec. 14, 1999, p.D1
*New York Times,* Aug. 31, 2002, p.D5; Sep. 6, 2002, p.D1
*Palm Beach Post,* Sep. 11, 2000, p.C1; Mar. 26, 2001, p.C1; Mar. 3, 2002, p.B7;
    Aug. 26, 2002, p.C1
*Rolling Stone,* Sep. 27, 2001, p.48
*Sports Illustrated,* Feb. 21, 2000, p.R6
*Sports Illustrated for Kids,* July 1, 2002, p.41
*Tennis,* Dec. 2001/Jan. 2002, p.22; Feb. 2002, p.11; Apr. 2002, p.72; Sep.
    2002, p.48
*USA Today,* Dec. 21, 1999, p.C16; Feb. 9, 2001, p.C8; Mar 28, 2001, p.C10;
    May 9, 2001, p.C1
*Vogue,* Sep. 2001, p.472

## ADDRESS

Andy Roddick
ATP Tour
200 ATP Tour Boulevard
Ponte Vedra Beach, FL 32082

## WORLD WIDE WEB SITES

http://www.andyroddick.com
http://www.atptennis.com
http://www.usopen.org

# Photo and Illustration Credits

Mildred Benson/Photos: The *Blade*/Diane Hires; The *Blade*; Book cover from THE SECRET OF THE OLD CLOCK by Carolyn Keene (NANCY DREW MYSTERY SERIES ®). NANCY DREW and all related characters and images are copyright and registered trademarks of Simon & Schuster, Inc. All rights reserved. The classic hardcover editions of these Nancy Drew titles are available from Grosset & Dunlap, an imprint of Penguin Books for Young Readers.; The *Blade*; © ABC Photo Archives; The *Blade*.

Alexis Bledel/Photos: copyright © The WB/Lance Staedler; copyright © The WB/Mitchell Haddad; copyright © The WB/Andrew Eccles; Ron Phillips/copyright © Disney Enterprises, Inc. All rights reserved; copyright © Disney Enterprises, Inc. All rights reserved.

Barry Bonds/Photos: AP/Wide World Photos; S.F. Giants; Otto Greule, Jr./Getty Images; Al Bello/Getty Images; AP/Wide World Photos; Jed Jacobsohn/Getty Images; Donald Miralle/Getty Images; Brian Bahr/Getty Images.

Kelly Clarkson/Photos: Kevin Winter/FOX; Ray Mickshaw/FOX; Jim Ruymen/Reuters/TIMEPIX. CD covers: RCA Records. Logo: FOX.

Vin Diesel/Photos: AP/Wide World Photos; Bob Marshak/2001 Universal Studios; courtesy Columbia TriStar Home Entertainment; copyright © 2000 New Line Productions, Inc. Courtesy New Line Home Entertainment. DVD covers: *The Fast and the Furious* courtesy Universal Studios Home Video; *The Iron Giant* program content, artwork and photography copyright © 1999. Courtesy Warner Home Video.

Michele Forman/Photo: AP/WideWorld Photos.

Sarah Hughes/Photos: AP/Wide World Photos; Ezra Shaw/Getty Images; Clive Brunskill/Getty Images; AP/Wide World Photos; Doug Pensinger/Getty Images.

Enrique Iglesias/Photos: Andrea Comas/Reuters/TIMEPIX; copyright © Bettmann/CORBIS; AP/Wide World Photos. CD covers: *Enrique* copyright © 1999 Interscope Records; *Escape* copyright © 2001 Interscope Records.

John Lewis/Photos: AP/Wide World Photos; copyright © Bettmann/ COR-BIS; copyright © Spider Martin Collection (page 142); AP/Wide World Photos; copyright © Bettmann/CORBIS; copyright © Flip Schulke/COR-BIS; Dirck Halstead/TIMEPIX

Andy Roddick/Photos: Andrew Wallace/Reuters/TIMEPIX; Eric Gaillard/ Reuters/TIMEPIX; Clive Brunskill/Getty Images; Jeff Gross/Getty Images.

# How to Use the Cumulative Index

Our indexes have a new look. In an effort to make our indexes easier to use, we've combined the Name and General Index into a new, Cumulative Index. This single ready-reference resource covers all the volumes in *Biography Today,* both the general series and the special subject series. The new Cumulative Index contains complete listings of all individuals who have appeared in *Biography Today* since the series began. Their names appear in bold-faced type, followed by the issue in which they appear. The Cumulative Index also includes references for the occupations, nationalities, and ethnic and minority origins of individuals profiled in *Biography Today.*

We have also made some changes to our specialty indexes, the Places of Birth Index and the Birthday Index. To consolidate and to save space, the Places of Birth Index and the Birthday Index will no longer appear in the January and April issues of the softbound subscription series. But these indexes can still be found in the September issue of the softbound subscription series, in the hardbound Annual Cumulation at the end of each year, and in each volume of the special subject series.

## General Series

The General Series of *Biography Today* is denoted in the index with the month and year of the issue in which the individual appeared. Each individual also appears in the Annual Cumulation for that year.

## Special Subject Series

The Special Subject Series of *Biography Today* are each denoted in the index with an abbreviated form of the series name, plus the number of the volume in which the individual appears. They are listed as follows.

| | | |
|---|---|---|
| **Adams, Ansel** . . . . . . . . . . . . . . . . . | Artist V.1 | (Artists Series) |
| **Cabot, Meg**. . . . . . . . . . . . . . . . . | Author V.12 | (Author Series) |
| **Chan, Jackie**. . . . . . . . . . . . . . . . | PerfArt V.1 | (Performing Artists Series) |
| **Fauci, Anthony**. . . . . . . . . . . . . . | Science V.7 | (Scientists & Inventors Series) |
| **Moseley, Jonny** . . . . . . . . . . . . . . | Sport V.8 | (Sports Series) |
| **Peterson, Roger Tory** . . . . . . . . . | WorLdr V.1 | (World Leaders Series: Environmental Leaders ) |
| **Sadat, Anwar** . . . . . . . . . . . . . . . | WorLdr V.2 | (World Leaders Series: Modern African Leaders) |
| **Wolf, Hazel**. . . . . . . . . . . . . . . . | WorLdr V.3 | (World Leaders Series: Environmental Leaders 2) |

## Updates

Updated information on selected individuals appears in the Appendix at the end of the *Biography Today* Annual Cumulation. In the index, the original entry is listed first, followed by any updates.

**Arafat, Yasir** . . . . . . . . . . . Sep 94; Update 94; Update 95; Update 96; Update 97; Update 98; Update 00; Update 01; Update 02

**Gates, Bill** . . . . . . . . . . . . Apr 93; Update 98; Update 00; Science V.5; Update 01

**Griffith Joyner, Florence**. . . . . . . . Sport V.1; Update 98

**Sanders, Barry** . . . . . . . . . . Sep 95; Update 99

**Spock, Dr. Benjamin** . . . . Sep 95; Update 98

**Yeltsin, Boris** . . . . . . . . . . . Apr 92; Update 93; Update 95; Update 96; Update 98; Update 00

# Cumulative Index

This cumulative index includes names, occupations, nationalities, and ethnic and minority origins that pertain to all individuals profiled in *Biography Today* since the debut of the series in 1992.

Aaliyah . . . . . . . . . . . . . . . . . . . . . . . . . Jan 02
**Aaron, Hank** . . . . . . . . . . . . . . . . . . . Sport V.1
**Abbey, Edward** . . . . . . . . . . . . . . WorLdr V.1
**Abdul, Paula** . . . . . . . . . . . Jan 92; Update 02
**Abdul-Jabbar, Kareem** . . . . . . . . . . Sport V.1
**Aboriginal**
    Freeman, Cathy . . . . . . . . . . . . . . . . . . . Jan 01
**Abzug, Bella** . . . . . . . . . . . . . . . . . . . . Sep 98
**activists**
    Abzug, Bella . . . . . . . . . . . . . . . . . . . Sep 98
    Arafat, Yasir . . . . . . . . . . . Sep 94; Update 94;
       Update 95; Update 96; Update 97; Update
       98; Update 00; Update 01; Update 02
    Ashe, Arthur . . . . . . . . . . . . . . . . . . . . Sep 93
    Askins, Renee . . . . . . . . . . . . . . WorLdr V.1
    Aung San Suu Kyi . . . . . Apr 96; Update 98;
       Update 01; Update 02
    Banda, Hastings Kamuzu . . . . WorLdr V.2
    Bates, Daisy . . . . . . . . . . . . . . . . . . . . . Apr 00
    Brower, David . . . . . WorLdr V.1; Update 01
    Burnside, Aubyn . . . . . . . . . . . . . . . . Sep 02
    Calderone, Mary S. . . . . . . . . . . . Science V.3
    Chavez, Cesar . . . . . . . . . . . . . . . . . . . Sep 93
    Chavis, Benjamin . . . . . . . Jan 94; Update 94
    Cronin, John . . . . . . . . . . . . . . . . WorLdr V.3
    Dai Qing . . . . . . . . . . . . . . . . . . . WorLdr V.3
    Dalai Lama . . . . . . . . . . . . . . . . . . . . . Sep 98
    Douglas, Marjory Stoneman . . WorLdr V.1;
       Update 98
    Edelman, Marian Wright . . . . . . . . . . Apr 93
    Foreman, Dave . . . . . . . . . . . . . . WorLdr V.1
    Gibbs, Lois . . . . . . . . . . . . . . . . . WorLdr V.1
    Haddock, Doris (Granny D) . . . . . . . Sep 00
    Jackson, Jesse . . . . . . . . . . Sep 95; Update 01
    Ka Hsaw Wa . . . . . . . . . . . . . . . . WorLdr V.3
    Kaunda, Kenneth . . . . . . . . . . . WorLdr V.2
    Kenyatta, Jomo . . . . . . . . . . . . . WorLdr V.2
    Kielburger, Craig . . . . . . . . . . . . . . . . Jan 00
    Kim Dae-jung . . . . . . . . . . . . . . . . . . Sep 01
    LaDuke, Winona . . WorLdr V.3; Update 00

Lewis, John . . . . . . . . . . . . . . . . . . . . . Jan 03
Love, Susan . . . . . . . . . . . . . . . . Science V.3
Maathai, Wangari . . . . . . . . . . . WorLdr V.1
Mandela, Nelson . . . . . . Jan 92; Update 94;
    Update 01
Mandela, Winnie . . . . . . . . . . WorLdr V.2
Mankiller, Wilma . . . . . . . . . . . . . . . Apr 94
Martin, Bernard . . . . . . . . . . . . WorLdr V.3
Masih, Iqbal . . . . . . . . . . . . . . . . . . . . Jan 96
Menchu, Rigoberta . . . . . . . . . . . . . . Jan 93
Mendes, Chico . . . . . . . . . . . . . WorLdr V.1
Mugabe, Robert . . . . . . . . . . . . WorLdr V.2
Marshall, Thurgood . . . . . Jan 92; Update 93
Nakamura, Leanne . . . . . . . . . . . . . . Apr 02
Nkrumah, Kwame . . . . . . . . . WorLdr V.2
Nyerere, Julius Kambarage . . . WorLdr V.2;
    Update 99
Oliver, Patsy Ruth . . . . . . . . . . WorLdr V.1
Parks, Rosa . . . . . . . . . . Apr 92; Update 94
Pauling, Linus . . . . . . . . . . . . . . . . . . Jan 95
Saro-Wiwa, Ken . . . . . . . . . . . . WorLdr V.1
Savimbi, Jonas . . . . . . . . . . . . . WorLdr V.2
Spock, Benjamin . . . . . . . Sep 95; Update 98
Steinem, Gloria . . . . . . . . . . . . . . . . . Oct 92
Teresa, Mother . . . . . . . . . . . . . . . . . Apr 98
Watson, Paul . . . . . . . . . . . . . . WorLdr V.1
Werbach, Adam . . . . . . . . . . . . WorLdr V.1
Wolf, Hazel . . . . . . . . . . . . . . . . WorLdr V.3
Zamora, Pedro . . . . . . . . . . . . . . . . . Apr 95
**actors/actresses**
    Aaliyah . . . . . . . . . . . . . . . . . . . . . . . . . Jan 02
    Affleck, Ben . . . . . . . . . . . . . . . . . . . . Sep 99
    Alba, Jessica . . . . . . . . . . . . . . . . . . . . Sep 01
    Allen, Tim . . . . . . . . . . . . Apr 94; Update 99
    Alley, Kirstie . . . . . . . . . . . . . . . . . . . . Jul 92
    Anderson, Gillian . . . . . . . . . . . . . . . Jan 97
    Aniston, Jennifer . . . . . . . . . . . . . . . . Apr 99
    Arnold, Roseanne . . . . . . . . . . . . . . . Oct 92
    Barrymore, Drew . . . . . . . . . . . . . . . . Jan 01
    Bergen, Candice . . . . . . . . . . . . . . . . Sep 93
    Berry, Halle . . . . . . . . . . . . Jan 95; Update 02

# CUMULATIVE INDEX

181

199

# CUMULATIVE INDEX

# CUMULATIVE INDEX